The Poets' Quill

*The Wit, the Wisdom,
And the Wacky Side of
Indiana's Remarkable Poet*

Grandpa Moses

authorHOUSE

AuthorHouse™
1663 Liberty Drive
Bloomington, IN 47403
www.authorhouse.com
Phone: 833-262-8899

© 2021 Moses L. Hochstetler. All rights reserved.

No part of this book may be reproduced, stored in a retrieval system, or transmitted by any means without the written permission of the author.

Published by AuthorHouse 10/18/2021

ISBN: 978-1-6655-2984-6 (sc)
ISBN: 978-1-6655-2982-2 (hc)
ISBN: 978-1-6655-2983-9 (e)

Library of Congress Control Number: 2021912494

Inkwell & feather quill art by Ashley L Hochstetler

Print information available on the last page.

Any people depicted in stock imagery provided by Getty Images are models, and such images are being used for illustrative purposes only. Certain stock imagery © Getty Images.

This book is printed on acid-free paper.

Because of the dynamic nature of the Internet, any web addresses or links contained in this book may have changed since publication and may no longer be valid. The views expressed in this work are solely those of the author and do not necessarily reflect the views of the publisher, and the publisher hereby disclaims any responsibility for them.

CONTENTS

Blessed Curse 1
The Poet's Quill 2
Software 3
Wonder In Their Eyes 4
My Proposed Epitaph 5
The Royal Rose 9
Cherry Blossoms 10
The Tulip Is the Prettiest 11
Orchids Laced With Dew 12
The Lily 13
Marigolds 14
Confession 15
Jack-In-the-Pulpit 16
The Dandelion 17
Under the Lilac Bush 18
January, January 21
February Creeps In 22
March Is a Merry Melody 23
April's Relief 24
The Mystical Month of May 25
The Waltzing Month of June 26
Fireflies of July 27
Lazy Days of August 28
September Skies 29
Lovely October 30
Come November 31
December Wonderland 32
When the Geese Fly By 33
Old Man Winter 34
The Shepherd 37
No Balm In Gilead 38
Mumbo Jumbo 39

Mists of Mandalay	41
Queen Jezebel	42
Peace In Bozrah	43
Scarfing At the Squill	45
The Sailboat Cindy Lou	49
Captains In the Army	50
A Good Many Creatures	51
The Harvest Unicorn	53
Haunted House On Sycamore Street	54
The Mouse In the House	56
Old Jack Frost	59
Fussy Fugal	60
Heaven In the Cradle	61
The Measly Little Mouse	62
Say No To Drugs	66
Breathless	69
Whispers of the U-Creek	70
The Butterflies	71
Dawning	72
The Princess' Wedding Dress	73
Irreverence	74
Sparrow's Two-step	75
Wild Country	76
Beauty Around Us	77
Rainbow	78
Aunt Matildy's Soup	81
Adam's Debacle	83
Boondoggle Bash	84
Aloysius Can't	85
When Rosie O'Riley Cleans the House	86
Portly Peter Applegate	88
Camel Joe Browne	90
Scarecrow	93
Take A Pill	94
Limericks	96
The Blessings of Heaven	99

We Thank the Lord God	100
The Hands of the Potter	101
I Seek a City	102
Love Profound and Deep	103
My Hour of Prayer	104
Song of Sarah's Handmaid	105
May You Possess	107
Millennial Sonnet	108
Slaughter of the Midianites	109
Silence The Weapons of War	110
The Lord's Passover	111
The Captain of Our Ship	113
The Bells of Victory	115
For Want of Blessed Things	117
Cherish Every Gifted Moment	118
The Luciferic Cherub	119
Little Seeds	123
The Day of the Cavalry	124
The Iron Beasts	125
The Sage of Tara Hill	126
Spell of the China Sea	128
The Gentle Years	129
The First Marathon	130
The Red Brick House	132
The Widow Mattie Rhodes	133
The Old Wood-Stove	134
Shiloh	135
Ode To An Ancient Spiel	136
Your Love Gift	139
Passing Flowers	140
What Love Is	141
My Darling Rose	142
Island of Relief	143
Neath the Portals of Love	144
You and Me	145
Come dance With Me, Amanda Wells	147

My Butterfly of Love	148
A Tribute To My Love	149
Lights That Shine From Paradise	150
When I least Expected It	151
The Dagger's Edge	152
Love Rekindled	153
Marriage	154
Rendezvous With Life	157
The Glory of War	158
Beneath the Sod	160
Beneath November's Moon	161
Only Cowards leap	162
Shorty	163
The Questions I Keep Asking	164
As a Lighthouse Stands	165
Of Willow and of Wren	166
Bad Billy	169
The Cool Dude	170
Song of the Lonely Heart	172
Who Would Give Drugs To A Child?	173
The Man In the Cardboard Box	174
Monument of Death	175
A Person Is a Person	176
Rest In Peace	179
"DAD"	181
Mother's Love	183
Resurrection	184
Gifts To be Treasured	185
Morning Brings the Sunshine	186
My Blood, My Bones, My Brother	187
My Sister, My Friend	188
The Sleeping Seed	189
A Cottage Small	193
Sonnet of Peace	194
Rural Charm	195
The Valley of Saint Joe	197

O For a Moment 198
Home In Kosciusko... 199
As a Dream Dies 203
As the River Flows 204
Howl of the She-Wolf... 206
Come To Us.. 208
Home of the Native...210
The Tippecanoe..211
How To Rate and Judge Poetry 212

BLESSED CURSE

From my pen the ink is flowing,
Forming lines of rhyming verse;
Lunacy and wisdom mingle
In a kind of blessed curse.

From an endless well the words spring,
Gushing from the heart and soul;
E'er in all my night and daydreams
Does this passion take its toll.

Grappling me to cadent meter,
Chaining me to shades of truth;
Trembling, I lie prone and helpless,
Spent upon the shores of youth.

Now at last the well is empty;
I, the pauper, in the hearse.
Poets dead are more impressive,
'T is a kind of blessed curse.

THE POET'S QUILL

The Poet's quill
Rich observations trace
Upon the bonded leaf.

Soft sonnets weave
Through life to leap with joy,
Or weep in common grief -

To touch the heart
And pluck the stringless harps
Of feelings long denied.

Fine ballads dance
Upon the writer's page:
To song of virgin bride,

To battles won,
To heroes never known,
To dreams, to dreams that die -

But all is lost
To all posterity
Before the critic's eye.

SOFTWARE

If the bugs of contradiction
Fill my mind with reams of doubt,
If I think the truth is fiction
And that facts are sauerkraut;
Then somehow this diskette matter
Driven in between my ears,
Was programmed with dither-dather
And my brain has slipped its gears.

But if I should choose to program
Factual data bit by bit,
Onto my memory's ROM or RAM
Where I can soon recall it;
This computerized contraption
Storing megabytes of writ,
Yields with electronic action
Valued little gems of wit.

WONDER IN THEIR EYES

When I was just a young lad
And barely into school,
Just learning to speak English;
For at home we spoke what some
Would call a lower German,
I was so painfully shy,
And stumbled over my words,
Too embarrassed to answer
Even when asked a simple thing
Like "What is your name?"
Or "How old are you, son?"
'Twas then I had a wondrous dream
That I was out in the barn
Standing atop a granary bin,
And down below me, gathered there,
A huge expectant crowd all looking up at me
With wonder in their eyes,
As from my mouth there flowed
A stream of poetry so delightful
With effortless ease and joy,
As to amaze myself and them.
It wasn't until much later
After I had lived two-score,
That I found that somewhere deep
Inside there was indeed a fount
Of words and phrases, rhymes
And reasons, just waiting to
Flow out and to be shared with
That huge expectant crowd;
And though I'm not there
Inside that barn looking down,
I do see the people of my dream...
    With wonder in their eyes.

MY PROPOSED EPITAPH

Here lies a great master of rhyme,
Of meter, of words, and of mirth;
He might have been famous in time,
Had he not taken leave of this earth.

But his words will live on through the years,
And arise like a ghost from the past;
No need to shed crocodile tears,
For his work shall be vaunted - at last.

FLORAL ARRANGEMENTS

THE ROYAL ROSE

The rose is the flower of all flowers
And we would do well to emulate her.

To the child she inspires awe and wonder,
To the youth she wakens love,
To the married she renews ardor,
To the poor she offers riches,
To the sick she offers well-being,
To the broken-hearted she offers cheer,
To the despondent she offers hope,
To the angry she offers sweetness,
To the enemy she offers peace,
To the bereaved she offers condolences,
And for the dead she fondly remembers.

She is truly royal in her demeanor
And regal in her disposition,
And yet she is as much at home
With the pauper as she is with the king;
For with all her overflowing goodness
She is condescending to no one.

CHERRY BLOSSOMS

Every spring the cherry tree
Puts on her wedding gown,
Embroidered with the morning mist
And laced with feather-down.

Blushing as a virgin bride
Unveiled before the groom,
With heaven's scent embracing her
From each enamored bloom.

Cherry blossoms lift the heart
On merry wings of cheer,
To make all sad and melancholy
Moments disappear.

THE TULIP IS THE PRETTIEST

The daisy is a little coy,
The rose a bit too proud;
The lily sits too quietly,
The orchid is too loud,
The peony presumptuous,
The lavender is shy;
The poppy is a platitude
Reaching for the sky.
The marigold is blooming late,
The daffodil too soon;
The tulip is the prettiest
To grace the afternoon.

ORCHIDS LACED WITH DEW

Who milked the morning sunrise
And purloined rainbow hues,
To tint your formal garments
In ultraviolet blues?

Who spun the finest Siam silk
To cover up your crown;
Who splashed the scent of angels' breath
Upon your evening gown?

Who gathered up the moonbeams
And took the starlight dust,
To sprinkle on your petals
And shine your lovely bust?

God made the finest flowers
To cheer us when we're blue,
But none are more delightful than
The orchids laced with dew.

THE LILY

The lily is the empress
Of the valley and the lea;
The guardian of the morning light,
The mistress of the sea.

The queen of all the flowers
That grow on every isle;
The country buds and blossoms,
The orchids of the Nile.

MARIGOLDS

If you see the marigolds
In confusing rank and file,
And you see their heads all bobbing
As they snicker with a smile;

It's because with orange and yellow,
And a splash of copper-brown,
Those conniving little bandits
Have each commandeered a crown.

CONFESSION

I saw within the meadow lands
As I was passing by,
Flirtatious little darlings
By fields of wheat and rye.

They looked at me, they winked at me,
They hoped that I would stay;
To dance among the dandelions
And romp upon the hay.

They begged of me, they tempted me,
I must not acquiesce;
But I am just a mortal man,
And thus I must confess:

I held them close unto my breast,
I smelled their sweet perfume -
The day I passed the meadow lands
And saw the daisies bloom.

JACK-IN-THE-PULPIT

Jack-in-the-Pulpit
Never a dull wit
So humbly bows to pray,
Preaching a sermon
Of General Sherman
In shades of blue and gray.

The Honey Suckle
Will never buckle
To serve Emmanuel,
The crimson flower
Of passion and power
Seduced her with his spell.

The African Violet
Listening while it
Sits on a greenery pew,
Her tears of sorrow
Are gone tomorrow
Though baptized with the dew.

The Lily in white
Does walk in the light
To keep all her garments clean;
For washing in water
The Master Potter
Has chosen her as His queen.

THE DANDELION

The dandelion is a pretty little flower,
A pretty little flower is he.
He is bright and pert as he stands alert
In a sea of greenery.

The dandelion is a dandy little royal,
A dandy little royal is he:
An aristocrat with a feathery hat
That he flaunts indignantly.

The dandelion is a cunning little devil,
A cunning little devil is he.
He is unafraid of the mower blade
As he stands and winks at me.

The dandelion is a hardy little fellow,
A hardy little fellow is he.
You can cut his crown when the sun goes down
And he's back for morning tea.

UNDER THE LILAC BUSH

Ah, the scent of lilacs blooming, how it brings forth joyful tears,
How it stirs up youthful memories of the long gone yesteryears,
Of a bush of lilacs thriving plush and thick in our front lawn,
Intertwining branches growing ever shading on and on.
All the scented flowers sprinkled in profusion 'mongst the leaves,
With its mystical illusion of the tapestry it weaves
In a purple greenish pattern as a covering for my den;
My perfumed Shangri-La that I would visit now and then.

'T was a welcome place and hideout from all troubling kith and kin,
Where I could make my peace with heaven and could make my peace within,
In that sanctuary lilac with its branch encircling wreath;
Giving comfort, peace and solace from its refuge underneath.
Often I would take my troubles and my childish grief and pain
To that haven 'neath the lilacs, both in sunshine and in rain.
There my pensive brow would soften, there my aches would fade away,
There my tear-eyed face would brighten in the coolest shade of day.

My dear mother, heavy laden with her worries and her cares,
Would so quickly smile with pleasure when I plucked the flowers there,
And I'd bunch them all together in a wild abandoned way,
For the sight of lilacs blooming would soon melt her frowns away;
And though I'm grown now, and older, yet my griefs are scarce denied,
And with heaviness the burdens I have often heaped inside
Until I think of shaded lilacs plush and thick upon the lawn,
Intertwining branches growing ever shading on and on.

TIMES AND SEASONS

JANUARY, JANUARY

"January, January, come on in,
Welcome back, where have you been?"

"Out to seek a wind to blow,
A pond to freeze, a coat of snow;

Out to form some blizzard skies
Before the temperature will rise.

"January, January, come on in,
Welcome back, where have you been?"

"Up to where the arctic bends
Around a circle and descends;

Up to where the jet stream wends
To where that circle never ends.

FEBRUARY CREEPS IN

February crawls in, falls in, bawls in,
Comes in with the wind, and the rain, and the snow;
February skips in, trips in, whips in;
You never can tell: whether fast, whether slow.

February sleeps in, creeps in, leaps in;
Blows in with a gust, and a shriek, and a howl.
February rumbles in, stumbles in, tumbles in;
You never can tell: weather fair, weather foul.

February walks in, stalks in, squawks in,
Comes in with the sun or a blustery cloud.
February sails in, gales in, wails in;
You never can tell: whether meek, whether proud.

MARCH IS A MERRY MELODY

March's a merry melody
Of piccolos and flutes,
With winds that whistle cheerfully
Accompanied by lutes.

A violin reverberates,
A cello laughs with glee;
A ukulele frets with joy
Through branches of a tree.

Rhythmic drum-beats can be heard
Along the city street;
A dozen boots in unison,
A dozen dancing feet.

The north wind hums in minor key,
The west wind sings with mirth;
March's a merry melody
In tune with mother earth.

APRIL'S RELIEF

April comes as a relief,
A bursting out
Of bud and leaf,
An urge to shout;
A welcome back to southern ports
For those who loathe the winter sports.

April comes as falling rain,
A southern breeze,
The sweet refrain
Of birds and bees;
Abundant flowers in the wild,
A promise to a little child.

April comes as swallows fly
On feathered wings
Up in the sky,
And awesome things:
Clouds that wear a golden crown,
Trees that bloom a cashmere gown.

THE MYSTICAL MONTH OF MAY

May is a mystical heavenly dawn,
Lighting up a green felt lawn.

May is a time to welcome back
Butterflies in a multi-pack.

May is a palette of flowers in bloom,
Dancing in the winds of nature's loom.

May is a couple humming a song
With the warblers singing along.

May is a childhood jubilee;
Skipping along so merrily.

THE WALTZING MONTH OF JUNE

Hear the chorus of the songbirds
In the waltzing month of June!
See the sun in splendor setting,
See the golden rising moon!

Breezes softly greet the morning,
Sparkling dew bejewels the grass;
Pink and purple clouds embellish
Eastern skies for lad and lass.

Smell the flowers in the meadow
Glowing in the sun at noon;
Daisies dance while violets polka
In the waltzing month of June!

See the wedding couple beaming,
See the kissing bride and groom,
As they meet up by the altar
In this waltzing month of June!

FIREFLIES OF JULY

July, July, the month that I,
Pick the cherries for the pie,
See golden wheat, oats, and rye,
See fireflies go flying by.

July, July, in high degrees,
Sweat is flowing with such ease;
Seek the shade beneath the trees –
Linger, linger, feel the breeze.

July, July, the night goes by,
Early morning sun is high,
Late the sun will leave the sky;
Sink and slowly, slowly die.

LAZY DAYS OF AUGUST

O hazy, hazy, August morning;
Giving sailors ample warning
From a sky that's turning red.
Dew upon the clover clinging,
Tides are up, the birds are winging
Out to sea in search of bread.

O crazy, crazy, days of August:
Skies of blue, and sometimes robust
Storm clouds roll in from the deep;
White-capped waves will pound the shoreline,
Standing close, you'll feel the salt-brine
Sting your eyes and make you weep.

O lazy, lazy, August nightfall,
Hear the lonely whippoorwill call
As the light turns ebony;
Wrap the world in purple velvet,
Sprinkled with the diamonds, well set
High above the emerald sea.

SEPTEMBER SKIES

The sapphire skies of September's early mornings
Speak to me of autumn prematurely born;
A tint of amber in the emerald leaves
Behind a veil of iridescent mist.

The fire of diamond dust flaming in the sunrise,
Dew of rainbows clinging to the willow's breast;
Unwilling to abandon summer's passion,
The south wind whispers soft romantic prose.

Rapt overtures of songbirds spill into the daybreak,
Cornucopia harvests fill the fields with gold;
The sweetest wine ferments when August folds
Her garments with intoxicating charm.

Hold back the winds that kiss Yukon's crystal dome,
Herald first the blazing of the lusty fall.
Pause - hail the time when all the world's a wonder;
All prayers unspoken - hushed in reverent awe.

LOVELY OCTOBER

October is such a lovely month,
The trees turn into gold;
And yellow, orange, and fiery red,
As autumn days unfold.

October is never long enough,
It quickly passes by;
Too soon its days are history
And do you wonder why?

October clings to summer days
Without the burning heat,
And keeps the frigid winter months
At bay beyond her feet.

COME NOVEMBER

The trees have all shed their robes,
The stoves are filled with ember;
The orchards are all stripped of fruit -
Come November.

The darkness creeps in earlier,
The warmth stays in September;
My overcoat comes out to stay -
Come November.

The robins' nests are empty now,
The winds howl for December;
Cumul'imbus clouds turn gray -
Come November.

DECEMBER WONDERLAND

Glitter, sparkle, in the night,
Beneath December's pale moon light.
Above the sky is crystal clear;
A million stars appearing near.

Reach and touch the Milky Way,
Stroke the dippers on display,
Tread the path Orion takes;
Quiet, else the hunter wakes.

Clouds now hide December's moon;
North winds howl an arctic tune;
Snow will blanket evergreens,
White-outs hide the wintry scenes.

Come, December, come our way;
We won't hasten you away -
In this winter wonderland,
We can see our Maker's hand.

WHEN THE GEESE FLY BY

Coming from the cold north,
Forming a vee,
Beating their wings
Austerely:
South to a pleasant
And balmier clime;
Sounding their requiem.

The dandelions'
And the thistles' down;
Long ago buried
In the fallow ground.
The last of the mournful
Autumn winds sigh,
When the geese fly by.

Drumming to the heart's beat,
Drumming "defeat",
Sounding taps for
The fall's retreat.
Ashes in the fireplace
Flicker to a flame,
Sparked by the passing game.

The sky turns gray
And the grasses fade,
The frost stays white
In the morning shade.
The last leaves of summer
Turn brown and die,
When the geese fly by.

OLD MAN WINTER

The snow is melting on the hills,
The ice is full of doubt;
The winds are blowing softer now
And less inclined to pout.

A pride of daffodils arise
To strut their frocks of green;
The birds are flying from the south
And singing for the queen.

The cows are lowing in the stalls,
The horses kick the air;
Old man winter's weak and wane,
And rocking in his chair.

MYSTICAL MUSES

THE SHEPHERD

He arises as a common man
Before the wheat turns;
Before the corn tassels,
Before the tender grapes turn
Blue upon the vine.
He appears incognito
In the light of morning;
In the shrine of the temple,
Among the sheep of his
Most pleasant pasture.

"Awaken!" He shouts,
"For the dawn has arrived!"
The sheep are scattered
To the four winds of heaven.
The wolves have devoured
The young lambs of the hills,
Yearlings bleat in the valley
Of thistles and thorns,
For the grass is withered
In the fields of Shiloh.

He comes to prune the vines
That the hireling shepherds
Have trampled into the mire.
Let not your hearts be troubled;
He arrives with healing hands
Dripping of holy anointing oils:
Cinnamon, myrrh, cassia,
Olive and sweet calamus.
The spirit of Elijah will shake
The mountains of Sierra

NO BALM IN GILEAD

Sweet jubilation Paeans sweep the soul
Of every merry youthful lad,
But how the heart's nostalgia weeps
Great wells of tears for Gilead.

Past anticipations quickly flee away
To leave us empty shells of hope,
Though now and then a glimmering light
May cause us to sedately grope:

To seek that fount which flows through youth eternal;
A soothing solace left behind
To salve the bitter memories
That plague and torture peace of mind.

Sweet jubilation paeans sweep the soul
Of every merry youthful lad,
But all who seek such ancient joys
Will find no balm in Gilead.

MUMBO JUMBO

High on a wooden pedestal,
Carved from a sacred cinder block;
Two eyes stare from a Brahman bull,
Standing on a wedge of temple rock.

Worshipping Baal in the holy land,
Holy water in the desert sand;
Much too deep to understand,
The mysteries of the Babel land.

Mother of harlots, heavenly queen,
The birth of a chosen infant son;
Kneel to the god of the evergreen,
Deep in the heart of Babylon.

Hocus pocus magic tricks,
Phallic symbols, mystic sticks;
Mumbo jumbo voodoo fix,
All together in a ritual mix.

Holy vestments, priestly gowns,
Hallowed days and solemn vows.
Hollow churches in their towns;
Sanctimonious "better than thous."

Bow to the queen of Babylon,
Bow to the brothel shrine salon;
Bow to the prostitutes' icon,
Here in the land of Babylon.

Cross on the steepled belfry tower,
The little Lord in the manger view;
Tarot cards and the witching hour,
Worshipping Baal and Jesus too.

Ishtar weeps in the Shinar land,
Evergreens in the desert sand;
Much too deep to understand,
The mysteries of the Babel land.

MISTS OF MANDALAY

Where the moon casts forth a shadow
On the hills beyond Khartoum;
There the mists of Mandalay enshroud
The portals of the tomb.

Arise, my love, to meet me
In the prism of the night;
Ere the sun impales the Cypress tree
With beams of brilliant light.

Sing the melody with passion,
Play the harp in minor key;
Let us dance beneath the Milky Way
Upon the silvery sea.

Arise, my love, to greet me -
From the graveyard of the deep;
Where the ashes of your body rest
On tides of timeless sleep.

Let the moon cast forth her shadow
On the hills beyond Khartoum,
Let the mists of Mandalay unlock
The portals of the tomb.

Arise, my love, to treat me
With the essence of your smile -
Let my heart, triumphant, welcome
You; rejoicing all the while.

QUEEN JEZEBEL

She comes with the winds of the morning,
Riding high on the crest of the tide;
They kiss by the moon at the dawning,
With blood dripping red at her side.

She chants her dark secrets of Egypt,
To sounds of a cold iron bell,
Her eyes have the depths of a sea crypt,
Her heart beats a rhythm from hell.

Her flames lick his thighs with desire;
Melting all his resolve with her heat.
She sets his libido on fire
As sparks will set fire to wheat.

Her lips are the lips of an adder,
Her tongue is the tongue of a snake;
Enthralled by her eyes when he met her,
But crushed by the scorn in her wake.

She gives him the look of a harlot,
As she ties the cold noose with her wit.
Her words draw him into her slip knot;
She seduces him into her pit.

She leaves with the winds of the evening
As he falls with a wound in his side;
Her knife buried deep leaves him grieving,
His blood dripping red in the tide.

She chants her dark secrets of Egypt,
To sounds of a cold iron bell;
As he sinks to his grave in the sea crypt,
He whispers "My Queen, Jezebel."

PEACE IN BOZRAH

A Metaphor

As I walked the distant seashore
Of the ancient sands of time,
The winds above the gentle waters
Whispered this inviting rhyme.

"Deep within your anguished bosom
Sad and painful sorrows hide;
You will find your peace in Bozrah
Sheltered in the shifting tide."

Frightened, I alone did wander
Beaches fathomless and vast;
Through millenniums uncensored,
Through the eons of the past.

To the present moment's pounding
Of the surf upon the reef;
Pounding with surrealistic
Indignation fueled with grief.

Tortured to the depths of madness,
Tethered with a mortal chain;
Dashed in pieces, wounded, bleeding,
On the shoals of kindred bane.

There persuasive whitecaps whispered
Words that I had heard before:
"You will find your peace in Bozrah,"
Hence I heard those words no more.

For the endless sea dispersing
Every tear within its brine;
Beckoned me, intoxicating
Me with waves of brandywine.

And it drowned my pain and sorrow,
And it swallowed fear and qualm;
And I found my peace in Bozrah
In a timeless sea of calm.

SCARFING AT THE SQUILL

Way back in the time when the Moogles ruled the world,
And the moons blazed yellow-gold, and slippery silver-pearled
O'er the swank switchy grass beneath the valley Myst,
Back when young Yllissa had her gyddy-eyed tryst,
And her dudly caught her wysting with her sizzles unfurled,
Wysting with Garbanza, who she par-broil kyst.

Then her dudly stook her out to his brumbelary shed,
And he beat her pansy bushka till she was gnarly dead.
Ladies didn't wyst in those dailies back then;
Kept their sizzles hidden from all the wankie men -
Till the blue-bells pringled, till bedding-vows were said;
Didn't broil-kyss till the moons were black again.

Garbanza ran back home to his grovel on the shill,
Ashamed to show his face again, ashamed to show it still;
Till all the little telly-moons succumb their mellow light,
And the billows buff "swooshy" through the switchy at night -
Then Garbanza will come duncing out, scarfing at the squill,
Fitching for another chance to flick Yllisa's kyte.

That's the way it was when the Moogles ruled the world,
When the moons blazed yellow-gold, and slippery silver-pearled.
Wankie men came duncing out, fitching for a chance,
To wyst a young gyddy-myss and husque her circumstance;
Scarfing at the squill to see her sizzles unfurled,
Hoping that her dudly wouldn't squork an avalanche.

FOR THE YOUNG AT HEART

THE SAILBOAT CINDY LOU

'T was the dreadful swelling sea
That sank the sailboat Cindy Lou.
Her captain brave as brave could be
Was Captain Harley Barleybrew.

His first mate Jack Aristocrat
Was thin and more than half-mast tall.
The second mate with sailor hat
Was Hurly Burly Butterball.

The damsel fair with hair of gold,
With lips of glossy cherry-red
And skin of ivory, I am told,
Was Namby Pamby Newlywed.

The little girl with lots of spunk,
With hair as black as starless night,
Who stowed away in someone's trunk,
Was Amorindy Mindy Mite.

The tossing sea and churning waves
Soon covered decks on fore and aft,
And all aboard went to their graves
Along with that poor sailing craft.

And so the boat, the men and dames
Were lost at sea without a trace,
But I can still recall their names
And see the fear on every face.

For I was there to see it all,
I took them out and wiped them dry;
And to the bedroom down the hall
Went boat, the crew, the dames and I.

CAPTAINS IN THE ARMY

The Earl of Kentucky
And the Duke of Tennessee,
Are captains in the army
Under Robert E. Lee.

They lead a great battalion
Of Virginia musketeers,
They're out to capture Sherman
With their Georgia volunteers.

They won't give up or leave their ranks,
Come join the marching band;
These mighty men of valor
Fight till victory's at hand.

They will march from Carolina
Up along the coastal plain,
They plan to chase Ulysses
Simpson Grant to Bangor, Maine.

They are decked with gold and silver
From their medals by the score;
Awarded for their bravery
In this cataclysmic war.

The Earl of Kentucky
Is a boy of only three,
And his five-year-old brother
Is the Duke of Tennessee.

A GOOD MANY CREATURES

A good many creatures
Lived with each other,
As artfully told by this rhyme.
They dithered and dathered,
They slithered and slathered;
Together they had a good time.

Two dogs and a cat, six geese and a rat;
A crusty old cow with no tail.
Three pigs with white spots,
Their tails tied in knots;
An old donkey tied to a rail.
A gander, a goat, whose pedigreed coat,
Had long ago lost its shine;
Four cackling red hens, ten rabbits and wrens
All got along just fine.
Then came a mouse, and a fat little grouse;
Together they made thirty-three.
The next afternoon came a ring-tailed raccoon
Who seldom crawled down from his tree.

A good many creatures
Lived on the same farm,
And for years there was ne'er any harm.
They pittered and puttered,
They littered and cluttered,
But alas, there was cause for alarm.

Two dogs chased the cat, six geese hissed the rat,
And the cow kicked over the pail.
Three pigs squealed accusing
The donkey of using
Their knots to play pin-on-the-tail.

The angry old gander got up his dander
And flapped at the pedigreed goat.
Four cackling red hens, ten rabbits and wrens
Poked fun at his dusty old coat.
The beady-eyed mouse told lies of the grouse
Who flew off to heaven knows where.
The 'coon had enough and packed up his stuff;
To leave his tree house swept and bare.

A good many creatures
Who'd lived with each other
Fought over who leaves and who stays.
They scattered and tattered,
They spattered and battered,
And soon they all parted their ways.

Two dogs coaxed the cat, six geese hailed the rat,
The cow put her milk in the pail.
The pigs and the donkey
Did a twist called "The Monkey"
And sang till their songs became stale.
The gander heaped praises that dazzled the blazes
Of all, but especially the goat.
The cackling red hens, the rabbits and wrens
Gathered 'round to admire his coat.
The beady-eyed mouse made friends of the grouse,
And asked her on over for brunch,
The raccoon came back to his tree-house shack,
For an open-house tea and for lunch.

A good many creatures
Made peace with each other
And smothered the smoldering fuel.
They chitted and chatted,
They knitted and tatted,
While adopting the golden rule.

THE HARVEST UNICORN

In the summer month of August
Or September's waning moon,
When the nights are warm and quiet
With no sound of lark or loon;
If you strain your ears to listen
By the fields of tasseled corn,
You can hear the padded hoof beats
Of the harvest unicorn;
And if you should be as lucky
As my cousin Robin Frye,
You might just get a glimpse of him
As he goes trotting by.
He will come up from the river
Where the tributary flows,
Treading softly for his breakfast
Long before the rooster crows.
If you ever hope to see him
You must rise before the dawn,
And sneak down to the corn field
Just as quiet as a fawn;
For the slightest tap or tinkle,
Or a sneeze, or half a cough,
And that fleetest of all creatures
Will go quickly dashing off.
So be careful to breathe easy,
Do not make the slightest sound,
Never mind that older people
Say there's no such thing around;
For the unicorn of harvest,
Though he's strong, and sleek, and bright;
Is not visible to grown-ups,
Only children in the night.

HAUNTED HOUSE ON SYCAMORE STREET

There is an old house on Sycamore Street,
All battered and peeled, and weather-beat,
With naught in the windows but shards of glass,
With nearly a decade of un-mown grass,
All overgrown with nettles and weeds,
Briars and thistles, and cocklebur seeds.
If you peek inside of the house by the door,
It's dark in there, and what is more:

It's haunted! Oh, yes,
That's what I've been told;
That's why it's still empty
And never been sold.

At night when the wind goes whistling through
There's moaning and groaning and cries of "woo!"
And high in the rafters so dark and still
A whisper is heard with a deadly chill,
And down in the basement dank and cold:
A squeak, and a creak; and a "bong" is tolled.
And somewhere way down in the mold and the must
There's blood mingled with dirt and dust:

And bodies! Oh, yes,
That's what they all say;
Dead, buried, and rotting
In oozy-wet clay.

One night when the moon was hid by a cloud,
When the dark was as dark as a dead man's shroud,
Rip snuck to that house on Sycamore Street,
What he saw that night put lead in his feet,
Turned his blood cold inside of his veins,
Seized up his joints in vices and chains,
And took his last breath with a rasping sound,
Then lowered him down into the ground:

He's buried! Oh, yes,
From head to his feet;
NOW RIP HAUNTS THIS OLD HOUSE
ON SYCAMORE STREET!

THE MOUSE IN THE HOUSE

A little mouse found an old house,
And crawled inside by a clock.
The mouse heard a noise;
Heard a TICKETY-TOCK!
The mouse sat quiet and shivered in shock,
Then ran in fright from the noise in the house,

What a noise! What a scare!

The mouse ran fast, but the rat saw the mouse.
"What is your hurry?" the rat asked the mouse.
"I heard TICKETY-TOCK inside that old house!"
The rat scratched his head
As he wondered at that,
And went on his way to look for the cat,

What a scandalous pair!

"Good day," said the rat
To the cat on that day,
"Just wait until you hear
What I have to say!
The mouse in the house heard a
TICKETY-TOCK, CLICKETY-ROCK!
And ran from the house
As he shivered in shock."

And the cat raised her hair.

The cat gave a "MEW!"
As she went on her way,
She saw a black dog out running at play.
"I have news you can use,"
Said the cat to the dog.

"The mouse in the house heard a
TICKETY-TOCK, CLICKETY-ROCK,
KA-BOOM, KA-BOP!"

And the dog raised his hackles.

"What!" cried the dog as he ran to the barn.
"Did you hear, did you hear,
Did you hear of the harm?
Of the mouse in the house who heard
TICKETY-TOCK, CLICKETY-ROCK,
KA-BOOM, KA-BOP, CLACKETY-CLANG
AND SMACKETY-BANG!"

And the cow tore her shackles.

"No!" said the cow. "What a sad tale,"
And she rushed to the horse
That was tied to a rail.
"Horse," said the cow
As she brushed past a bale.

"You must hear the sad tale
Of the mouse in the house who heard
TICKETY TOCK, CLICKETY ROCK,
KA-BOOM, KA-BOP, CLACKETY-CLANG,
WITH A SMACKETY BANG
FROM THE RAFTERS ON TOP!"

And the horse hung his head.

"What is wrong?" Asked the mouse
Of the horse that was sad,
"Haven't you heard?" groaned the horse,
As he shook his sad head.
"The mouse in the house heard a
TICKETY TOCK, CLICKETY ROCK,

KA-BOOM, KA-BOP,
CLACKETY, CLACKETY, CLACKETY-CLANG,
WITH A SMACKETY, SMACKETY, SMACKETY-BANG
FROM THE RAFTERS ON TOP!"

"And the poor mouse is dead."

"Not so," said the mouse
As his face turned red.
"That is absurd, that is NOT what I said!
I heard a noise just over my head,
A TICKETY-TOCK, and that's why I fled."
And with a huff the mouse
Went back home to bed.

So beware of what's said.

OLD JACK FROST

Somewhere within the Arctic realm
Beyond Saskatchewan,
There is a frigid land they call
The land of Neverdawn.
There in that dark and frozen waste
A prankish imp resides,
And every fall he scampers down
Those slippery slopes and slides.
He sneaks across the meadowlands
Amongst the grass and trees,
And paints a coat of crystal-white
On everything he sees.
He leaves a nip of winter chill
To play an autumn trick;
Some say his name is
"Old Jack Frost,"
And some say "Jack B. Quick."

FUSSY FUGAL

Fussy Fugal sits at the table,
Fussy Fugal still is unable
To eat his food with dignity.
To him it's just stupidity
To relish every morsel of meat.
"It's altogether too hot to eat!"
"Too cold!" "Too tough!" "Not salty enough!"
"Do I have to eat this awful stuff?"

Fussy Fugal picks at his food,
Making remarks repulsive and rude:
His salad is "Yuk!" his soup is "Scum!"
And his veggies have never yet been "Yum!"
Fuss, and fume, and fiddle around,
And then, when everyone else is done,
You hear this sad and mournful sound:

"I'm hungry, Mom!"

HEAVEN IN THE CRADLE

There's a peaceful nook,
There's a babbling brook,
There's the "coo" of a darling dove;
There's a bleating lamb
Wondering where I am,
There's an innocent's heartfelt love.
There's a golden curl,
There's a dimpled pearl,
There's a dream that an angel keeps;
There's a little bit of heaven
In the cradle where the baby sleeps.

There's honey and milk,
There's satin and silk,
There's a joy that can't be told;
There's a beaming face,
There's amazing grace,
There's a glory to behold.
There's a happy smile
With no hint of guile,
There's a sparkling jewel worth heaps;
There's a little bit of heaven
In the cradle where the baby sleeps.

THE MEASLY LITTLE MOUSE

Late in the evening
At half past nine,
I was sleeping sweetly
In this bed of mine.

I heard a little "knick, knick"
Coming from the door,
I waited for a minute
Then I heard it once more.

Now mind you, it wasn't
A "knock, knock" at all,
But a tiny "knick, knick"
On the door by the hall.

So I tip-toed down
To the door of my house,
And when I opened the door
In walked a little mouse.

With his duffel bag stuffed
In a galvanized pail,
With pince-nez glasses
And a shiny waxed tail.

A measly little,
Weaselly little,
Pink-nosed mouse.

"Do you s'pose you could let
Me in for awhile?
I'm all but worn out
'Cause I walked a whole mile.

It is cold out there
By the frosty moon,
And the cat and the owl
Want to eat me soon."

So I said "OK,
You can stay till spring,
But you have to leave
When the blue birds sing."

So he parked his pail
By the pantry door,
And his duffel bag
On the dining room floor.

He thanked me then
With the slightest bow,
With the wink of his eye
And a raised eye-brow.

That measly little,
Weaselly little,
Pink-nosed mouse.

Now it wasn't very long,
'Bout a week or two,
And his wife moved in,
And his children, too.

And his kin folks came
From the woods out back,
And his country friends
By the railroad track.

And his mother-in-law
With her city friends,
Came from a neighborhood
That never ends.

And the nerve of those mice
And their love-sick mates,
They begged for dinner
By tapping their plates.

And they ate my food,
All my flour and rice;
My cookies and my crackers
They wiped out twice.

Those measly little,
Weaselly little,
Pink-nosed mice.

When I went to bed
I could hear them chew,
On my brand-new rugs
And my carpets, too.

And they scampered about,
And they scratched the walls,
And they partied all night
In the closets and halls.

But one such night
As I slept in bed,
I heard a soft "knuck, knuck,"
Sounding in my head.

Then I heard it again,
What could it have been?
When I opened the door
A cat walked in.

With a hand-basket full
Of pink and yellow yarn,
And a straw-tick pillow
She had filled in the barn.

"Do you s'pose you could let
Me sleep on your mat?
And I'm really quite starved,
I could eat a whole rat!"

Now what do you all,
Everybody,
Think about that?

SAY NO TO DRUGS

Those drugs are dumb,
They're not so smart,
They make you numb,
They stop your heart.
Those drugs are worse
Than poison bugs!
Say YES to LIFE!
Say NO to DRUGS!

Those drugs are bad,
They make you cry,
They make you sad,
They make you die.
Those drugs are worse
Than poison bugs,
Say YES to LIFE!
Say NO to DRUGS!

Those drugs are sick
They give you pain,
They kill you quick,
They fry your brain.
Those drugs are worse
Than poison bugs,
Say YES to LIFE!
Say NO to DRUGS!

BEAUTY AROUND US

BREATHLESS

The brooding clouds of summer wear
A luminescent crown;
But when they show their colors off
They wear an evening gown.

The rainbow dons a summer wind,
And sits astride a hill;
A model posing for the paint,
Breathless, nude, and still.

WHISPERS OF THE U-CREEK

In the evening when the shadows dull
The harsh and glaring stress of the day;
When pillows melt the tensions away,
My heart steals back to an early age:

Back to the meadows where the U-Creek
Does softly whisper yesterday's words
Of carefree times and grazing herds,
Of barefoot boys and purple sage;

Back to meadows where the butterflies
Come back to taunt a ten-year-old,
Where bumblebees in their search of gold
Go wending through the timothy;

Back to a time when the summer months
Are filled with crickets and killdeer,
And the U-creek whispers into my ear:
"Come back to me, come back to me."

THE BUTTERFLIES

They dance upon the summer winds,
They kiss the budding rose;
They're such an inspiration for
The poets and their prose.

They flutter in the morning light,
They shimmer in the sun;
They leave the awe and wonder
Of the child in everyone.

A miracle as marvelous
And pleasing to the eyes,
As living diamond gemstones...
The lovely butterflies.

DAWNING

The amber glow of early morning light
Does warm the heart in ways we cannot say;
All frightful dreams that chill the darkest night
Are cast aside, and softly melt away,
To leave us with a brighter view and hope
Than things that we may face that could offend,
So we may have the strength to better cope
With bitterness, and let the anguish mend.
For dawning light does warm the heart and soul,
Extinguishing each sad or vengeful thought.
It spreads a blanket on the burning coal,
And cools the embers that the night has wrought.
So let us greet each day the Lord will give;
Embracing it as friends embrace, and live.

THE PRINCESS' WEDDING DRESS

Few, indeed, can hope to guess
What is this princess' wedding dress:
A fluff of dainty silken white,
A ruffled petticoat in flight,
Whispering quiet as angels' wings,
Draped in purple fit for kings;
A scepter blowing in the breeze,
No feathers, still it flies with ease,
Through hills and valleys,
Through the town,
Flies this princess' wedding gown.
It sails and seeks a fertile place
To rest its soft and royal lace,
And there it plants its tiny throne
To make all subjects wince and groan,
If they should dare to touch the crown
From whence we find............

The THISTLEDOWN.

IRREVERENCE

A grove of cottonwoods at rest
Upon a Sabbath day;
Whispering in somber tones
And bowing as to pray.

Beneath their leaves and limbs outstretched
In great solemnity,
The sassy little saplings dance
And play irreverently.

SPARROW'S TWO-STEP

A sparrow sits upon the eave
And chirps a cheerful "howdy do,"
Then fluffs and preens her feathered breast
And does her two-step dance routine.
She flits and flutters round about
And chirps again to say "adieu."
Then bowing low she spreads her wings
To exit left and leave the scene.

WILD COUNTRY

The flowers in the wild and the solitary place,
The Buttercups, Violets, and Queen Anne's Lace;
All the evergreen trees and the cottonwood coves,
The oak, the maple and the hickory;
I just love it here in the wild country.

The marshes in the meadows and the wet land swamps;
There's the hawthorn thicket where the bobcat romps.
See the fresh water fish in the rivers and streams;
The eagles soar over land and sea,
I just love it here in the wild country.

See the snow in the mountains and the waterfall;
Hear the loons on the lakes, the whippoorwill call.
Walk the pine needle carpet of the forest floor
Where the whitetail deer roam wild and free;
I just love it here in the wild country.

Now taste the sparkling water, breathe the fresh clean air;
Walk the wilderness path of the wolf and bear.
Eat the nuts and the berries; watch the setting sun,
Light a crackling fire 'neath the hemlock tree;
I just love it here in the wild country.

BEAUTY AROUND US

There's the smell of budding clover in the meadows,
There's the scent of violets blooming in the glen;
In the valley daisies peek out from the shadows
Of the willows as if chicks beneath the hen.

See the beauty of the lilies in the morning,
See the grace that they display for everyone;
See the colors of the rose adorn the evening,
As you watch the glory of the setting sun.

O the wonder of the ravens and the eagles,
Of the swallows as they glide upon the air,
Hear the singing of the birds out in the pine trees
And the whistling of the whippoorwill so fair.

See the butterflies go gliding on the breezes,
See the summer clouds billow in the sky,
See the leaves in autumn turn to gold and amber
And the yellow daffodils when spring comes by.

There's the beauty of stars up in the heavens,
There's the beauty of the land and of the sea;
Yes, there's beauty in the universe around us
That the Lord our God has made for you and me.

RAINBOW

A flash of brilliant summer-green,
A kiss of heaven-blue,
The red, orange, and yellow sheen
Of sun on morning dew.

The lavender the lilacs love,
In spring when flowers bloom;
The rainbow weaves the colors of
This world on her loom.

THE LIGHTER SIDE

AUNT MATILDY'S SOUP

We would gather 'round the table
At my aunt Matildy's place,
And she'd spread her bestest dishes out,
And napkins trimmed with lace;
Then she'd take the biggest kettle
Off the stove a-boiling hot,
And she'd fill our bowls to brim full
With that stuff from that old pot.
I'd a-reckon sure as shootin'
It was like the time before,
When she served that same concoction
And I spilt it on the floor;
For it tasted so disgusting
That I claimed I'd never stoop,
So low that I would eat again
My aunt Matildy's soup.

Now I know that Aunt Matildy
Must Have done the best she could,
And my mamma complimented her
And said "How awf'ly good!"
And my dad was quick to state that
"It's quite an undertaking."
But when they got away from her
They'd start to belly aching –
"And why?" my dad would always say,
A loos'ning up his belt,
"Why do I always leave her place
The worst I ever felt?"
He didn't have to answer that,
I knew it was that scoop
That held too much, yes, way too much,
Of Aunt Matildy's soup.

She must have added noodles made
Of eggs a mite too old,
And dried out bits of carrots that
Were crusted green with mold,
And I suppose she scraped the table
For a week or two, at least,
For scraps of beef and chicken bones
Not fit for man or beast,
And the smell of it was strangely like
The smell of spoilt meat -
So I ask you, no, I beg you,
Not to make me sit and eat
That gristly mix that gags you
And will knock you for a loop;
Not a solitary spoon full of
My Aunt Matildy's soup.

ADAM'S DEBACLE

Young Adam did live in the garden of Eden,
He must have been happy in there;
Reclining for hours 'neath heavenly flowers
And gathering fruit everywhere.

The Lord gave to Adam young Eve with her beauty
Who captured his heart with a smile;
With hugs and with kisses, such marital blisses
Abundantly rich and worthwhile!

Together they lived in the garden of Eden,
It must have been beautiful there;
The grass a bit greener, and Eve, if you'd seen her,
Would quite leave you gasping for air.

Such radiant beauty, such charm and charisma,
Her hair blowing wild in the breeze;
Sweet orchids and honey, it's really quite funny,
How men can be won with such ease.

But all was not well in the garden of Eden,
For Eve soon gave heed to the snake;
And she, being baited, was quickly persuaded,
Not knowing her life was at stake.

But Adam, poor Adam, gave in to her wiles,
And taking the fruit from her hand;
Disarmed by her greeting, took pleasure in eating,
Right there in that beauteous land.

So God drove them out of the Garden of Eden,
And left the whole world to grieve;
And Adam, as all men do blame it on women,
Did blame the debacle on Eve!

BOONDOGGLE BASH

I never heard such a boondoggle bash,
As I heard when "Slick" Coogin; young, fickle and brash,
Proposed a proposal down on the state floor
To start each day half-an-hour sooner'n before.
Two-year McDoogle was next on his feet,
And he stoked and bellowed the coals to white heat:
"I second the motion to get something done,
If you're looking for votes then I'll give you one!"
"Hold on to your horses, hold on to your blouse!"
Yelled a seasoned old statesman esteemed by the House,
"I've been here two-score and I never have heard
A proposal that sounds so insanely absurd!"
The hoots and the heckles poured forth from the floor
Until Congressman "Doc" Gooseman stormed out the door.
Finally the Speaker brought order to bare
By breaking the gavel and pounding his spare.
A hush and a silence enveloped the crowd
As he called on old Hardigan, august and proud;
Who giving opinions in very few words
Emphatically spit out "This bills for the birds!"
They haggled, and haggled, and haggled some more
With a hullabaloo even worse than before;
And they fought the next day, and the day after that,
Till all the reps wearied of where they all sat.
So the highway bill was shoved to the back,
And a tax-relief package soon derailed the track;
A new code of ethics was pushed to the side,
And a great many other bills withered and died -
'Cause they're still there today in their pin-striped grays
Split right down the middle with "ayes" and with "nays"
And who knows who wins or who even keeps score
Of all the boondoggles down on the State floor?

ALOYSIUS CAN'T

Take warning from this sober tale
Of Aloysius Gant,
Who as a child in diapers still,
Learned how to say "I can't."
The old folks thought it cute and laughed,
When Mom said "hush-a-bye,"
And he would say with puckered lips,
"I can't, I got to cry!"
When Aloysius was quite young,
His mom would rave and rant:
"Do this! Do that! You lazy boy!"
And he'd just say "I can't."
No different as a grown man,
He never could recant;
His neighbors often asked his hand,
He'd say "I simply can't."
His wife would always work so hard,
She'd run, and sweat, and pant.
She'd ask him "Will you please help out?"
He'd say "You know I can't."
And even when the minister
Implored him to repent,
That man would hem and haw around
And say "I really can't."
When finally Aloysius died,
And faced the pearly gate,
Saint Peter shook his head and said
"You've met an awful fate."
And all those who had entered in
Took up this sing-song chant:
"We'll spend our time in paradise!"
But Aloysius can't.

WHEN ROSIE O'RILEY CLEANS THE HOUSE

When Rosie O'Riley cleans the house
It's quite a sight to see;
When Rosie O'Riley cleans the house
It's clean as clean can be.
She fluffs the pillows, makes the beds,
And wipes the dirty walls;
She sweeps and mops and cleans the floors
And shines the dingy halls.
She dusts the furniture with ease
And makes the woodwork glow;
When Rosie O'Riley cleans the house
It's really quite a show.
She rushes here, she rushes there,
And quickly does her work;
She whistles tunes, she sings and croons,
And makes the coffee perk;
And when she takes a morning break
To fix the breakfast meal,
She sighs and flicks her hair aside,
And says "It's no big deal."

When Rosie O'Riley cleans the house
It's always neat and tidy;
Not a speck of dirt throughout the house from
Saturday through Friday.
She cleans the windows, spiffs the glass,
And makes the mirrors new,
She washes, dries, and folds the clothes,
And does the dishes, too.
She mows the lawn and rakes the leaves
And bags them all away;

Trims the hedges nice and neat,
And never asks for pay.
She rushes here, she rushes there,
And makes her mother proud,
She whistles tunes, she sings and croons
And ne'er complains aloud;
Just smiles and flicks her hair aside
And says "It's no big deal,
Some days I do a whole lot more,
It's all in how I feel."

When Rosie O'Riley cleans the house
Her day has just begun,
She plows the fields and plants the corn,
And still her work's not done.
She cleans the stables, milks the cows,
And beds them down at night;
She strains the milk, and takes the cream,
And churns it thick and white.
She heaps it on the pies she bakes
And serves them to her guests;
Then gets their coats and sees them off
Before she goes and rests.
She rushes here, she rushes there,
And seldom gets much sleep.
She whistles tunes, she sings and croons,
And earns her board and keep.
She smiles and flicks her hair aside,
And says "It's no big deal."
Some day someone will marry her
For more than sex appeal!

PORTLY PETER APPLEGATE

Portly Peter Applegate,
Born a month and two weeks late.
Roly-poly, something's wrong,
Ten pounds wide and ten pounds long!
Ten quarts milk to drink each day,
Six pints cream and four pints whey,
Seven yokes of wild-goose eggs
And still for more he pleads and begs.
Custard pudding, ginger snaps,
Applesauce to fill the gaps,
Bowls of corn-mush, liverwurst,
Until his tummy nearly burst.
Hundred-two pounds overweight,
Portly Peter Applegate.

Portly Peter Applegate,
For his lunch was never late.
Twice as round as he was high,
Ate three pans of pizza-pie:
Two loaves bread with oleo,
Spinach greens to help him grow,
Five bowls soup, a roast beef shank,
A draft of beer from Pappy's tank,
A pound of cheese, a glass of wine,
Cloves of garlic, eight or nine,
Stacks of pancakes tall and thick,
The way he eats just makes me sick!
Twice a hundred overweight,
Portly Peter Applegate.

Portly Peter Applegate,
Sought a wife and sought a mate.
He found a girl with steady job
But stood her up for shish-kebab.
To satisfy his appetite
He snacks by day and snacks by night:
Jugs of cider, legs of lamb,
Plates of boiled smoke-house ham,
Sauerkraut and chocolate cake,
Cherry tarts and slabs of steak,
To name a few things that he had,
And still he asks his mom and dad:
"How did I gain so much weight?"
Portly Peter Applegate.

CAMEL JOE BROWNE

His rump was catawumpus,
His legs were knotty pine;
And if you took a compass,
His "north" was out of line.
He had a naked belly
And lacked a proper gown;
His flaming eyes were cherry pies:

Mean Camel Joe Brown.

He wore a yellow blanket,
A bridle draped his head;
His water, when he drank it,
"He slurped," his master said.
His feet were wide and clumsy,
His nose would spook a clown;
And when he spit he'd score a hit:

The Camel Joe Brown.

I dickered with his master,
To get to Timbuktu.
He said "You'll get there faster
If he belongs to you."
I bought him for a shilling,
Two farthings and a crown,
He cleared his throat; a motor boat:

That Camel Joe Brown

We took a crooked by-way,
Across the desert sand,
He never did it my way
When riding over land.
His "hump" was high and mighty,
His forehead formed a frown:
And when he ran the wind would fan

Past Camel Joe Brown.

Two bandits stood to rob us;
A pistol in each hand;
Joe kicked and made a ruckus,
And filled their eyes with sand.
I doubled up with laughter
As we came near the town;
He cracked his lip and let her rip:

This Camel Joe Brown

We formed a bond for ever
As we hit Timbuktu;
He licked my face so clever,
His tongue was two-foot-two.
I told that dromedary
I'd never let him down;
He chuckled twice, he's mighty nice:

My Camel Joe Brown

We went to board a ship deck,
The captain said "No way!
He'll surely cause a ship wreck,
We have no camel hay!"
Joe dove into the water,
I thought that we would drown;
No moments lost, the sea was crossed

  On Camel Joe Brown

We made our home in Dover,
I sent old Joe to school;
But he became a rover
And broke the truants' rule.
He ran around with drifters;
The "ne'er do wells" of town -
They thought him "cool" - that silly fool

Bad Camel Joe Brown

Soon Joe got hooked on hemp pot,
And chain-smoked cigarettes;
He made a mint as mascot,
But lost it all on bets.
His body filled with cancer,
We had to put him down;
It hurt me so to see him go –

Poor Camel Joe Brown

SCARECROW

He wears a stocking cap of red,
And gloves of white and blue;
His hair is yellow straw of wheat
Still damp with morning dew.

His eyes are bleak and rather drawn,
His beard a shuck of corn;
And still he wears the overalls
He wore when he was borne.

He stands out near the garden fence
All sober and astute;
He does his job around the clock
Though blind, and deaf, and mute.

TAKE A PILL

Do you suffer from a cold?
Are you getting sort of old?
Is your head wrapped tight in chains,
Pounding with incessant pains?

    Take a pill.

Take a red or yellow tablet,
Take a blue or greenish cap,
Just wash it down with water
Then go take your daily nap.
It's so easy when your queasy
And you feel that you could die;
It will make you feel much better,
It will lift your spirits high;
It's a wond'rous panacea
For the fever or the chill –

    Take a pill.

Are you feeling down and out,
Do you suffer from the gout?
Are your joints as stiff as boards?
Are your kidneys swollen gourds?

    Take a pill.

Take a pill the morning after,
Take a pill the day before,
If your bottle becomes empty
You can always ask for more.

It's so easy when you're queasy,
And you feel that you could die,
It will make you feel much better,
It will lift your spirits high;
You can cover up the symptoms
When you're down or when your ill -

    Take a pill.

Has your get up gone from you,
Have you caught the dreaded flu?
Does your riser rise no more,
Do you lack the will to score?

    Take a pill!

Take a pill to energize you,
Take a pill to slow you down,
Take a pill to make you sleepy,
Or to wake you come the dawn;
It's so easy when you're queasy,
And you feel that you could die,
It will make you feel much better,
It will lift your spirits high;
Get your pharmacist to help you
Get you hooked against your will -

    Take a pill!

LIMERICKS

There once was a mistreated goose
Who suffered incessant abuse,
Until quite as by chance,
She snipped off the pants
Of the culprit and pinched his caboose.

There once was a hoot owl that hooted,
But the best hoot he hooted was muted;
So he thought he would howl,
That old hooty owl -
But try as he might, he just tooted!

There once lived a man named Tobiath
With an ego the size of Goliath.
Said he - "I appear to
Be great to live near to."
But his neighbors all say that "He liath!"

There lived an old maid with a purse,
Who saved every dime, and what's worse,
She hoped when she died,
That she'd get a free ride,
In the back of a limousine hearse.

SPIRITUAL PERSPECTIVES

THE BLESSINGS OF HEAVEN

As a friend I do wish you
The best of life's blessings
And freedom from suffering and pain.
May your prayers and oblations,
As blooms of carnations,
Flourish in sunshine and rain.

May the blessings of heaven
Be showered upon you
With favor from God and from man.
May you harvest with pleasure
The fruits of your labor
To share with whoever you can.

May the dew in the morning
Refresh and delight you;
May your days be filled with great peace.
May your nights without number
Be filled with sweet slumber;
Your dreams filled with hope never cease.

May your mate and your children
Bequeathed and beloved
Be cherished as jewels set in gold.
May your joy blend with laughter,
Both now and hereafter,
As the days of your life unfold.

WE THANK THE LORD GOD

We thank the Lord God
For these blessings in life:
The fruits of our labor
Gleaned without strife,

A bountiful harvest,
Sunshine and rain,
Children and laughter,
Love without pain;

A place to call home,
Chairs, table, and bed,
A comf'table spot
For my weary head;

Friendship and kinfolk,
Neighbors next door;
There's no need to ask
For anything more.

THE HANDS OF THE POTTER

May the blessings of God be upon you,
Your faith be alive and complete:
To keep you in touch with the Master,
Delivering you from defeat.

May the angels of heaven be with you,
To guide every step that you take;
To watch for all dangers around you,
While sleeping and while you're awake.

May the Spirit of God be inside you
To fill you with faith and with hope;
To grant you both peace and contentment,
And give you the courage to cope.

May you rest in the hands of the Potter,
Conformed to the shape of His will;
So when he returns in His power -
He finds you conformed to it still.

I SEEK A CITY

I seek a city with gates of pearl,
Built upon jasper, emerald and beryl;
A city with twelve gates in the wall
One hundred and forty-four cubits tall.
Where neither sun, nor light of moon
Is ever needed, night or noon:
For bright is He who dwells therein,
Free of darkness, free of sin;
A four-square city of purist gold
Where peace, and joy, and love unfold,
Where never a tear is shed in pain,
Where never a deed is done in vain;
No hunger, no want, no thirst, no fear,
A river of water crystal clear
Flowing from the throne of God,
Where sits the Lamb: the Shepherd's Rod,
The Fruitful Vine, The Living Key;
The Rock and Fortress safe for me;
Where grows a tree on either side
To heal the nations far and wide;
A tree of life with fruit for all,
For John and Peter, James and Paul;
For you and me if we abide
As His betrothed and lovely bride.
I seek a city not of this world,
Clean and precious, jeweled and pearled,
Where walk the ransomed free and blest;
And I, redeemed, an honored guest.

LOVE PROFOUND AND DEEP

A love that is profound and deep,
Who knows such love as this?
Who comprehends, who dares to reap
Such fruit of joyful bliss?

For has not God, who gave His Son,
Bequeathed His love to all -
To shed His grace on everyone,
To lift all those who fall?

For all have turned to lean toward sin;
All hearts have taken dirt;
And none can cleanse himself within,
Nor heal himself from hurt.

But this, a love profound and deep,
That's shed from heaven's throne -
Is worthy of our minds to keep;
All hearts to claim their own.

MY HOUR OF PRAYER

I call upon my Maker's name,
I feel His presence near;
My trouble lifts with His free gifts
Of mercy, love, and cheer.

The sweetness of the moment fills
My heart with joy divine;
With grace to please upon my knees;
His Spirit lifting mine.

The more I pray the closer still
I long myself to be;
My Father's clone, for Him to own,
And Christ to live in me.

To taste the hope, embrace the faith,
To walk in one accord;
Grant me the skill, the strength and will,
To follow my dear Lord.

To sip from His delightful cup,
His living waters share;
To give and take from heaven's wake
Within my hour of prayer.

SONG OF SARAH'S HANDMAID

My love and my lad of the Patriarch,
My son and my darling Ishmael;
The light in your eyes is turning dark
And your body grows faint and frail.

Come sit by my side as your heart grows weak,
Come sit by my side as you rest.
Together we God and mercy seek
As you lay your head on my breast.

If only the two of us hand in hand
Could give heed to the master's bell;
To dine and to dance in Canaan's land
And to drink from Abraham's well.

For Abraham's water is clean and clear
And quenches the smoldering coal;
It cools the ember of every tear
And refreshes the anguished soul.

Come lean on my bosom my hapless dear,
Come die in my arm's embrace;
For death from this dearth to us is cheer
And our joy is the burial place.

For the desert winds shriek and wail, my love,
And the owls and the cormorants cry;
And my heart pines away as the mourning dove
To see my sweet Ishmael die.

I will kiss all the sorrow from your face
And wet your dry lips with my tears;
Let us breathe our last farewells with grace
And soothe our last tremors of fears.

But Hagar distraught and weak with her dread
Could not bear the son's suffering and pain;
So Egypt's m'dam left him for dead
'Neath the shrubs of Beersheba Plain.

Now Ishmael cried unto God in the drought
And b'sought for his mother's despair.
A guardian angel hasted about
And delivered the languishing pair.

Then Sarah's hand maid did beautif'ly sing
This song to her son in the dell:
"Glory to God for the fresh water spring
Of Abraham's life-giving well."

MAY YOU POSSESS

May you possess the fearless heart,
The depth of strength, reserve of will,
The keen determination,
The swift and bold response to life
Unyielding and resolved;
May you possess the brave adamant

HEART of the LION.

But more than this, may you possess
The humble and the gentle touch,
The love and joy of living;
The tranquil and contented mind
With hope and faith devout.
May you possess the meek innocent

SPIRIT of the LAMB.

MILLENNIAL SONNET

The winds of change have never blown as strong,
The sun not shone with such an ardent glow
As soon will face earth's trembling mortal throng;
Once these millennial centuries flow
Into the clean and pristine virgin years
Of a new untarnished brilliant age
Where dreams can live, where living hope appears
To fill all hearts with peace, and fears assuage
To quell the cursed ravages of war;
An epoch with empathy's cutting edge
Behind each technocratic boardroom door;
And honor is due all at every age.
No winds of change have ever blown as strong;
No voices sung so eloquent a song.

SLAUGHTER OF THE MIDIANITES

A great host of an army spread out on the vale,
Their swordsmen and spear-men in wrought iron mail,
Their warriors on camels, their archers astride
Ten rows of horses one thousand feet wide.

Thus all Israel cowered in dread and great fear,
As Midian's army and Amalek drew near,
Devouring Israel as plagues of the Nile
Had devoured Egypt in wormwood and bile.

Hence Midia gathered their fruit and their grain,
Till Canaan was bare as the Saharan plain;
And Israel hid out in the dens and the caves,
And those who would not were soon captured as slaves.

But God sent forth Gideon, the arm of the Lord,
To deliver them out from the curse of the sword;
And with three hundred men, each with pitcher and lamp,
He descended upon that Amalekite camp.

Midst the blast of the trumpets, the shattering glass,
The multitude withered as dry desert grass;
And as swarms of locust do fall to the flame,
And more will fly forward, so they did the same.

Thus Midia perished that night on the vale;
The Amalekites ran to their death on the swale.
Shout! For the Lord will give victory and might,
To all those whose lamps will burn on through the night!

SILENCE THE WEAPONS OF WAR

An end, an end to the weapons of war:
To the sword, the spear, and the bow.
Stop the plunder, the blood, the gore,
And the death of friend and foe.
Quiet the muzzle of every gun,
The mortar, the volley of lead;
Quell all carnage under the sun,
The fear and the hopeless dread.

At peace, at peace ye nations of earth,
And good will from one to them all;
Host your neighbors from Paris to Perth,
And break down every wall.
Roll out the carpet, join hand to hand,
And embrace each ambassador;
Banish weapons from every land
And silence the weapons of war.

THE LORD'S PASSOVER

'Twas the Passover observance,
With its brightly shining moon,
As the thirteen of them gathered
In that little upper room.
There the Master became servant
To those men up in that hall;
Poured some water in a basin,
Washed the feet of one and all.
There He broke the bread asunder
And He told them all to take;
Passed the cup to His disciples
As He poured it for their sake:

For the memory of the Master,
For the worship of the Master,
And we never shall forget Him
For as oft as we partake.

In the night the crowd did gather,
Came to take the Son of Man,
Save the twelve - they all forsook Him,
Turned their faces and they ran,
While their Master did surrender
To that rabble-rousing mob;
To that cacophonous babble
Of those men that came to rob.
Then they mocked Him and they beat Him,
It was more than most could take,
And He took those stripes and suffering
For the rest of mankind's sake:

For the comfort of the people,
For the healing of the people,
And we show the Master's suffering
For as oft as we partake.

In Jerusalem, Judea,
On the outskirts of the town,
Came the Carpenter and Builder
With His sharp and thorny crown;
Struggling with His heavy burden
Weighing more than He could bear,
And they crucified the Master
There in Calvary's open air.
Yes, the day became as night-time
And the ground began to quake,
As this Jesus Christ of Nazareth
Spilled His blood upon that stake:

For the cleansing of the people,
For the saving of the people;
And we show Him that we love Him
For as oft as we partake.

THE CAPTAIN OF OUR SHIP

As many a soul sets sail this day
Of ladies, men and crew;
The morning sky is bright and fair,
The winds whisper adieu.

By nine the land beyond the wake
Is but a wisp of fog;
By ten the land is seen no more,
As notes the Captain's log.

An hour passes, still the sea
Is rolling gentle swells,
Much like a sleepy lullaby
Until the noon-time bells.

By one a sharp head-wind report
Unto the Captain's men.
By two the angry sea is like
A raging lion's den.

By three the sun is hid from view
And mountain-waves are seen;
The Captain yells "All hands below!"
His sense of safety keen.

How fierce the gale now whips the hull!
How fierce the water boils!
Below the demon-sharks await
To take the human spoils.

Above the Captain hears this cry
And prayer from every lip:
"Dear Lord we do of Thee implore
The safety of this ship!"

"Fear not," the trusty first-mate says,
"The Captain's at the helm,
And Him the wind and stormy sea
Can never overwhelm.

For He's a veteran of the waves,
He knows the shoals and keys;
He knows the depth of death and hell,
He knows the seven seas!

He'd give His life to save His foe,
How much think ye the more,
For friends and mates the likes of us
He'd reach the distant shore?"

The wailing wind at last is spent,
The roaring waves subside;
The vessel tempest-tossed is safe,
And all are safe inside.

Then scurry men and women all
To view the damaged deck;
To see the tackle strewed about
And see the twisted wreck.

They see the mast and anchor gone,
The hatch with broken lock;
And lo, the ship with unseen hands
Moored safely to the dock.

For aye, the Captain of our ship
Commands the winds and seas,
And safely brings those souls ashore
Who ask on bended knees.

THE BELLS OF VICTORY

Who will ring the bells of victory
In the heart of Beaulah-land?
   Who will smash the bluffs of Hermon,
   Who will glean the fields of Golan,
   Who will plant the rose of Sharon
In the midst of desert sand?

Who will sing the songs of David
In the heart of Judah-land?
   Who will cleanse the River Jordan,
   Who will banish gods of Dagon,
   Who will pluck the harps of Hebron
With the fingers of His hand?

Who will bring His crown and scepter
To reclaim Jerusalem?
   Who will build the wasted places?
   Who will feed the hungry faces,
   Who will create spirit-graces
And give each a diadem?

Who will ring the bells of victory
In the heart of Beaulah-land?
   He whose wine was made from water,
   He whose name is Master Potter,
   He whose anger waxes hotter,
And His sword is in His hand!

Who will gather sons and daughters,
To the heart of Judah land?
   He who kills the might high-beast,
   He who's ordained every high -feast,
   He who's known as heaven's High-priest
By the host angelic band.

Who will serve as kings and rulers
For the glorious beauty-land?
    He who's guided by the right source,
    He whose heart stays on the right course,
    He whose God comes on a white horse
    And his victory's at hand!

FOR WANT OF BLESSED THINGS

Joshua's battle cry resounds in every booth and tent:
And when the sun is risen, three thousand men consent
To smite the godless heathen on Isr'el's promised land;
To shed the blood of Canaanites upon the desert sand.

But Ai's men were waiting on Jordan's upper rim,
To chase the marching army back east to Shebarim;
And there the cunning Amorites reproached the mighty host,
By killing thirty-six of them before they reached their post.

Joshua's vaunted elders all groaned aloud, and cried:
"Would to God that we had stayed on Jordan's other side!"
But God appeared to Joshua, and told him to repent;
To seek the one responsible for this reviled event.

For sin is reprehensible, it breaks the nation's will,
It spills the blood of innocents, and slights the pauper's till.
Sin grieves the hearts of widows, and blinds the eyes of kings;
To leave the world destitute for want of blessed things.

Then Joshua cast the lot to find that cursed guilty man,
And found the son of Carmi; the covetous Achan.
Hence all of Israel stoned him in the valley of Achor -
Thus one gigantic heap of stones turned the tide of war.

Remember then should sin come by to knock upon your door,
Do not receive it in, my friend, to hide beneath your floor.
Be sure to shoo it far away, or let your feet grow wings,
Lest you receive a heap of stones, for want of cursed things.

CHERISH EVERY GIFTED MOMENT

Drizzle, drizzle, in the morning,
Gray clouds hanging low;
Cool and Misty fog is spreading
Where the wind does blow.

Dark and dreary, all the day long,
Making people sad;
But to those who love the rainy
Weather, hearts are glad.

Troubles daunt us, all the year long,
Worries leave us spent;
But to those who love the challenge;
Trials are heaven sent.

Iron always sharpens iron,
And shall hone the skill;
Striving hard against resistance
Only strengthens will.

Time is given as a present,
Live it to the full;
Cherish every gifted moment,
As a precious jewel.

Life can be a bumpy journey
Going up and down;
But the trip is worth the effort -
For the royal crown.

THE LUCIFERIC CHERUB

By the sea of glowing embers
Midst the realm of lights immortal,
Burning by the throne of Yahweh
(Great white shining throne of Yahweh)
Stood the Luciferic cherub
Cloaked in brilliant robes of rainbows,
Cloaked in hallowed words of wisdom
With his windless wings unfolded;
Spreading out and up and over;
Stood the Luciferic cherub
With a beatific brightness;
With a pious disposition
Midst the sea of angels waiting,
Midst the host participating,
Making music, music, music:
Making live symphonic music
With a blend of flutes and timbrels,
With a blend of golden bell-pipes
And a million spirits singing;
Singing rapturistic songs
In harmonious perfection,
With the hallelujahs ringing
From the choir celebratus:
With the sounds of strings vibrating,
With the sounds of pompous drum-beats,
With the blare of blasting trumpets,
With the clang of cymbals clashing!
-- And the melancholy lute –
For the host angelic spirits:
For the spirits, kindred spirits,
Myriad spirits filled with awe.

By the sea of glowing embers
Midst the realm of lights immortal
Stood the Luciferic cherub
Cloaked in brilliant shining brightness,
With the stars beneath his feet;
Stood the luciferic cherub
With a growing discontentment
Filled with envy, irksome envy,
Filled with overwhelming pride,
Filled with dark and dismal motives
Overshadowing his thinking,
Until all of him was bitter
And his bitterness turned sweet,
Until light became as darkness
And his darkness hid the light;
And his music turned macabre
And his dancing came from hell,
And a host of spirits followed
With their dancing, dancing, dancing
With a devilish delight,
And the host became demented,
And the host invaded Yahweh;
Fought the great majestic Yahweh,
(Who omnipotently reigneth)
Fought with Yahweh on His white throne;
And the ever living Spirit,
And the sea of living spirits
Spewed the darkness out forever
From the realm of lights immortal,
From before the throne of Yahweh
And the darkness was no more.

LONG AGO & FAR AWAY

LITTLE SEEDS

In the heart are etched the memories
Of golden moments past:
Of soft and gentle spoken words
And praise upon us cast,
Endearing smiles and helpful hands
Which often held our own;
The little seeds of selfless deeds
That long ago were sown.

In the heart are etched the memories
Of golden moments past:
Of lips that kissed away the tears
And hugs that held us fast,
Of warm and tender loving care
And sacrifices made;
The little seeds of selfless deeds
That grow while others fade.

In the heart are etched the memories
Of golden moments past:
Sweet memories that linger on,
As diamonds do they last.
A mother and a father's gift
Of time, in times of old;
The little seeds of selfless deeds
That shine as polished gold.

THE DAY OF THE CAVALRY

O glorious day, I wait to see your sun embark
Upon its journey through the lovely eastern sky.
I welcome you as meadows do the singing lark
And as flowers welcome dew when it is dry.

I can hear the bugles echo through the timbers
And a hundred bodies rise upon their feet;
All the campfires in the mist but glowing embers
Crackling low in beds of dying heat.

A hundred horses jostle in anticipation;
Snuff the air and paw the quivering sod.
Every man with musket takes his station
While lifting prayers heavenward to God.

In all the rank and file no idle chatter
Can cover up the heart's immortal cry:
"O Glorious day! What trivial matter
Will decide who shall live and who shall die?"

THE IRON BEASTS

The iron beasts of yesterday were seen
To follow paths of steel and ties of wood,
From east to west, through swamp, past evergreen,
O'er mountains, vales, and rivers' broad with flood.
From north to south and back up north again
They'd bellow blackened smoke and hiss their steam
While spewing forth their sparks, as tender men
Would feed these hungry beasts; each shift and team
Cooperate to keep them moving on,
So all could hear those wildcat whistles blow.
Throughout the day and from the dusk till dawn
They'd rumble, spit, and chug through rain and snow,
And from them you could tell the time and hour -
These beasts that went the way of dinosaur.

THE SAGE OF TARA HILL

From far away, across the sea,
There came a noble man;
He spoke of battles to the east
And mourned his country's fall;
He mourned his fellow kinsmen,
He mourned his father-land,
And raised his voice with eloquence...
Embracing Ireland.

From Palestine this sage did come,
The Sage of Tara Hill;
He brought along an entourage
And brought Emanuel's will;
He brought along a minstrel's harp,
He brought a granite stone;
A stone of great significance...
To plant on Ireland.

From Judah-land the prophet brought
The crown of Zedeki;
He brought the royal diadem
With princess TeaTephi.
He gave her hand to Herremon,
He placed them on the stone,
And crowned them as the king and queen...
Of ancient Ireland.

The sage was Ollam Fadhla,
His scribe was Simon Breck;
They built a university
On northern Tara Hill;

He trained young men as magistrates,
He trained them in the law,
He taught them jurisprudence...
To govern Ireland.

The stone is known as "Destiny,"
And in its presence were
The kings and queens of England
Established on the throne:
The sons of all the royals,
The daughters of the crown,
All trace their blood to Herremon...
And Tea of Ireland.

"As long as sun and moon endure,
The throne of David reigns,"
This is the solemn promise
Of God's own sacred word.
The stone: Jacob's Pillar Stone,
The harp was David's harp,
The prophet sent by God to place...
His throne in Ireland.

And so it is, today you'll find
In Lough Erne's cemeter',
On the Isle of Devenish,
Which claims bones at rest there
Are Jeremiah's bones,
The bones of old Fadhla,
The greatest legislator...
At rest in Ireland.

SPELL OF THE CHINA SEA

Under the spell of the China Sea;
The swell of her waves enchanting me,
The spray of her brine beckoning me:
The rise and fall of her tide once more,
The hiss of her surf upon the shore,
Whispering, whispering quietly -
Then calling my name with a thunderous roar!

Under the spell of the China Sea;
Intoxicating, embracing me,
Mesmerizingly swaying me:
With the tremulous touch of the hypnotist,
With a passion aroused by the evening mist;
Waiting there, waiting there just for me -
With love for the one she seductively kissed.

THE GENTLE YEARS

The gentle years come flooding into mind;
A time when car hop rest'rants were the rage -
When bobby socks and Hula Hoops defined
All those who wished to fit in with the age
Of juke box tunes and drive in picture shows,
When "45's" were in and "duck-tails" cool,
And corner stores were where the jet set goes
To have their fountain sodas after school.
The dime store was the only clothes boutique,
And groceries were sold by mom and pop,
When Elvis was the king, Sinatra sheik,
And everyone would "twist" down at the hop.
I wish I could go back there once again,
To take just one more stroll down mem'ry lane.

THE FIRST MARATHON

The sun above the sea was bright
Upon that August day,
Athenians, with Sparta's best,
Sought vict'ry from the fray
As fierce and hot the battle raged
Against the Persian force,
In the plains of Marathon,
The soldiers stayed the course.

The enemies were brutal,
But Athen's fought the more;
Resolved to push those fighting men
Beyond Aegean's shore.
With all their might they strove that day,
And drove the Persians out;
And when the sun was overhead,
Those Greeks begain to shout...

"We win!" they yelled with joyful shouts,"
We win!" they yelled with glee;
"We drove those bloody Persians out –
We won the victory!"
And so they had turned the tide
Where land the water meets,
But who would bring the news of this,
Back to Athen's streets?

"Pheidippides! Pheidippides!"
They clamoured loud and clear.
"He'll run the message back to town
So all the folks can hear
That we have won the battle,
That Sparta saved the day,
Freedom reigns throughout the land,
And Persia's turned away."

Across the plains of Marathon
Pheidippides did run,
Though summer heat was bearing down
From August's burning sun.
Along the dusty path he flew,
His strides a steady gate;
Through roughs, and rock impediments,
His speed did not abate.

Upon the walls of Athens,
Upon the towers ramp,
The watchmen stood and waited for
News from Athen's camp.
When, lo, there in the distance,
A cloud of dust arose;
A runner, yes, Pheidippides,
With steady gate now shows.

With bells of Athens ringing,
The trumpets sound the call…
"Come down to Athen's central square,
And hear ye one and all."
And so the people crowded in
To hear of Athen's fate,
As the courrier rushed within
The city's open gate.

"Rejoice!" he shouts, "Rejoice!" came from
The man Pheidippides,
"Rejoice! We win!" the runner says
And falls upon his knees.
And as a tree comes crashing down,
He falls upon his face…
Pheidippides, the mighty Greek,
Has run his final race.

THE RED BRICK HOUSE

The red brick house with the circular drive
Will always be home to me.
Surrounded by maples and spacious green lawn,
With song birds to wake me at breaking of dawn.
Lavender lilacs and flowers in bloom;
Fit for a princess; fit for her groom.
The red brick house with the circular drive
Forever my home will be.

The red brick house with the circular drive
Where loving hands cared for me.
Surrounded by brothers and sisters within,
A family including the cousins and kin
Where welcome guest could find table spread wide;
Fit for a prince and fit for his bride.
The red brick house with the circular drive
Forever my home will be.

The red brick house with the circular drive
Only in mind's eye to see.
Though bricks are now broken and house is no more,
My roots are still there, just inside the door
Where family shared love to make the heart sing;
Fit for a queen and fit for a king.
The red brick house with the circular drive
Forever my home will be.

THE WIDOW MATTIE RHODES

A lady filled with age, she was,
And spunky through and through;
She told us all to get in line,
This Mattie Rhodes I knew.

Filled with love of life, she was;
This widow "I can do."
She lived in her big farm house
Where all her substance grew.

Wrinkled in her face, she was,
And independent, too;
Still living by herself
When she was ninety-two.

Though burdened with the years, she was,
She fixed her meat and stew;
She cleaned the floors and cupboards
And made them shine like new.

Small and stooped with age, she was,
And still a trooper's hue;
Strong minded and determined;
And oft' times more than you!

Weathered and well-worn, she was;
Befitting like a shoe;
Undaunted by her problems,
She kissed them all adieu!

THE OLD WOOD-STOVE

I remember the days as a child I reclined
In a rocker beside the old stove;
That welcome old stove on the living-room floor,
That wood-burning, coal-burning, cast-iron stove
That crackled with fire in the pit of its core
With a savory smoke that I still can smell now,
Escaping from out of that cavernous door.

When the winters were cold and they cut to the quick,
And I shivered outside in the snow;
My fingers were numb and my swollen feet blue
In that nose-freezing, toes freezing, cold-as-ice snow,
It didn't take long to know just what to do:
Find a comforting place right next to that stove
With its fire belching smoke up the hot chimney flue.

So delightfully warm was that wood-burning stove,
So cheerful a place we could meet;
That welcoming stove on the living-room floor,
That heart-warming, soul-warming, bastion of heat,
That crackled with fire, that blazed with a roar,
From the red and orange flames of the logs and the coal
Flickering so bright through the eisenglass door.

And we all sat around that old living-room stove
Eating things that would just hit the spot,
While cold on the outside the winter winds blew,
That round-bellied, pot-bellied stove stayed hot,
And kept us all cozy and warm through and through,
As it sang us a song of a tropical breeze
To the tune of that wind-blown chimney flue.

SHILOH

Brother killed brother and kin here,
And friend killed friend as foe;
The wounded and dying did meet here
In the hills around Shiloh.

The blood of young men spilt here
To mingle with dirt and dew;
Was the sermon that was preached here
With the open grave the pew.

The widows were left to pine here,
The mothers were stricken with grief;
The singing of funeral songs here
Was sorrowful and brief.

The moon and stars shine soft here,
And the winds blow hushed and low;
For the dead have paid the price here
In the hills around Shiloh,

For the smoke that hung in the air here
Hangs thick in the air here still;
The echoes of guns can be heard here
In the quiet morning chill.

Memories never die here
Where these gallant men did fall;
The lessons etched in stone here
Are bitterness and gall.

Still the nation grows in grace here
And is cleansed white as snow;
From lessons taught and learned here
In the hills around Shiloh.

ODE TO AN ANCIENT SPIEL

The sputter and spit of the fiery pit
With a snarling flame of red,
As the hot coals glow
From the bellows that blow
In the blacksmith's humble shed.

A-rat-a-tat-tat, a-rat-a-tat-tat,
A-rink-a-dink-dink ado;
Is the sound that is heard
With never a word
For the likes of me or you.

The hiss of a cat from the water vat
As the iron cools to blue:
The steam and the smoke,
The grate and the poke,
The soot of the chimney flue.

The sweltering heat and the rhythmic beat,
The shower of sparkling steel;
The clash and clamor
Of anvil and hammer -
An ode to an ancient spiel.

SWEETHEARTS & BROKEN HEARTS

YOUR LOVE GIFT

The trellis roses bud in stark relief
Against the foliage of the garden fence;
Entwined with vines of green grape-leaf
Between the morning glory's opulence.
The scent of flowers fill the afternoons
With lovely musk and aromatic hint
Of dank equatorial jungle blooms,
And mellow tantalizing sage and mint...
I slowly lift my gaze aloft to see
Those love-filled eyes aglow upon your face,
And realize that no scent or sound could be
As sweet a thought as that of your embrace;
No sight as pleasant, and no rose could lift
My heart with such delight as your love gift.

PASSING FLOWERS

Shall love to us be whimsical and trite,
As passing flowers growing at our feet
That blossom in the cool of dawning light,
But fade away when smitten by the heat?
Our hearts but yesterday were filled with hope
Of life together, spent in gratitude
Of one another, but alas, we grope
For answers to our failure, and we brood
O'er things that should be put to rest, and cast
Aside as shards of some old broken urn;
We stumble at the errors of the past
To suffer as we bruise, we bleed and yearn -
If only we could gain the Spirit's gift
Of love restored; renewed to heal this rift.

WHAT LOVE IS

Love's a gentle hand in mine,
A stroll beneath the moon;
A whisper soft as Sherry wine
Sipped from an ivory spoon.

Love is taking off your shoes
And dancing in the rain,
With that special someone whose
Mere presence heals your pain.

Love is honor in a glance:
A wink, a smile, a nod;
Love is to a sweet romance
A little touch of God.

MY DARLING ROSE

Shall I compare you to a darling rose,
Whose fragrant bloom adorns the summer night;
A bud that shimmers with the dew, and glows
In gold and silver glints of soft moonlight?
The years have mellowed you as vintage wine
And graced you with this tender flower's hue,
To cause the face of your sweet love to shine
As though a rose had burst into review.
Though night be spent as darkness flees away,
The eastern sun will soon in gladness rise;
But still the silver of your hair will stay,
And glints of gold will glisten in your eyes.
Your petals never fade; your love still grows -
And I will always love my darling rose.

ISLAND OF RELIEF

Focused upon my hopes and dreams
As moments before me flee;
The rising of tomorrow's sun
Will bring them back to me.

Ever the silver cord be loosed,
Or ever the golden bowl
Be broken to a thousand shards,
And takes away my soul -

Give me confidence, my friend,
An anchor of love to keep;
A home and harbor safe and sound,
A place of tranquil sleep.

life is a fragile fleeting thing,
Awash in a sea of grief;
But love, if love be true, will be
An island of relief.

NEATH THE PORTALS OF LOVE

Sweet kisses of passion, the touch of a hand,
And tender words spoken, a small wedding band,
Whispered endearments, the sounds of a dove,
May be cherished forever 'neath the portals of love.

The birth of a baby, the purchase of toys,
The laughter of children, the sharing of joys;
The building of dreams is what I'm speaking of,
To be chrished forever 'neath the portals of love.

Sad moments of sorrow, dark days full of pain,
Heartaches, and teardrops that fall as the rain,
Forgiveness unmeasured, and all the above,
May be cherished forever 'neath the portals of love.

YOU AND ME

As together we renew our wedding vows
And remind ourselves of promises we made,
Let's rejoice in the time still remaining
And strengthen ties so love will never fade.

Still the honeysuckles grow in the valley
And the flowers bloom in spring for all to see;
The sun is shining brightly o'er the meadows
As the birds sing their songs for you and me.

The storm may gather darkness in the morning
And the clouds before the tempest swiftly blow;
We will look for our life's silver lining,
And find joy in the rainbow's crescent glow.

The noontime heat makes toil not so easy,
But fresh sparkling waters flowing through the lea,
Cools the brow and makes life more bearable
And the trees give their shade for you and me.

As we walk hand in hand down the pathway,
And the flowers of sweet youth begin to wane;
Though our dreams may not all find fruition,
The moments spent together are our gain.

Somewhere the awesome mountains reach for heaven,
Somewhere the white-capped waves crown the tossing sea,
But we will find our own sweet restful haven,
Right here at home together, you and me.

The sun is sinking slowly in the west
And paints the cloud-filled sky a thousand hues.
No doubt this is the best time of the day,
And so 'twill be for us if we so choose.

Let us harvest all our fruits as they ripen,
Let us gather in the grain before the cold;
Let us seek the well-being of each other,
And strengthen ties so love can shine as gold.

COME DANCE WITH ME, AMANDA WELLS

Come dance with me, Amanda Wells.
Come soothe your pulsing pain-filled heart;
Let all remorse from you depart.
Forget the past, forget regret,
Just tell me that you're glad we met;
Somewhere deep inside you dwells
A dance for me, Amanda Wells.

Come dance with me in ecstasy
To rapturous strains of violin.
Release yourself, your soul within;
Release the joy, release the song
There buried in your breast so long.
No kissing lips, no wedding bells,
Just dance with me, Amanda Wells.

Come dance with me, Amanda Wells.
Come free the quagmire in your mind
Of tangled memories entwined.
Come float across this waltzing sea
To wend and weave, to blend with me,
Till bliss your anguished bosom swells.
Come dance with me, Amanda Wells!

MY BUTTERFLY OF LOVE

A butterfly will fly to me some day,
And give me all I ever dreamed, and more;
To fill my heart with warmth, and wish to stay
To win me over to where I adore
And cherish her for who she is inside;
For beauty she displays from heart and soul,
And promise to be mine, and mine abide,
To fill the gaping emptiness, and hole,
That only one as sweet as she can fill -
So I await, and listen for her wings;
Although I reckon they be soft and still,
I know my heart will tell me when it sings.
If you should be the dream I'm dreaming of,
Please come to me, my butterfly of love.

A TRIBUTE TO MY LOVE

Her face is like a lamp that shines at night
To light the blackness of a darkened room;
Her eyes are eyes of kindness, sparkling bright;
I know her voice could cheer my deepest gloom.
Her smile, as sweet as honey from the bees
That gather nectar from the clover fields.
To walk as graceful as she walks with ease,
And spread the sunshine she so gently yields,
Must be a gift bestowed upon the few;
And rarely seen by men throughout their days -
For surely angels must be jealous, too,
That they can't match the beauty she displays.
If it was up to me I'd surely place
Her on a pedestal in silk and lace.

LIGHTS THAT SHINE FROM PARADISE

With love, and love's devotion dwell:
Two hearts betrothed, a wedding bell,
A hand in hand, an honored ring,
Respect for each in everything.

Encouragement, a mercy seat,
And service at the other's feet -
With willingness unhampered by
The years that pass beneath the sky.

And so, at last, when both are old,
The love is strong, enduring, bold;
The ties that bind: untarnished steel -
The rudder firmly guides the keel.

Within the spheres of those sweet eyes
Are lights that shine from paradise.

WHEN I LEAST EXPECTED IT

As a cool breeze in the heat of summer,
You came into my life when I least expected it;
Standing there as a lone palm in an oasis:
Elegant, with kindness in your hazel eyes
That met my own with a soft glow of acceptance
And humility that quite disarmed me.

Your voice carries the warmth of an afghan
crocheted from the finest mohair,
And strokes me as softly as a violin
Concerto in a minor key,
Performed in a rose garden
Under a full August moon.

Your smile lights up my life as the morning
Sun after an April shower. Your presence
Is as cool sweet wine in a dry season.
Your laughter plays upon my heart strings,
Harmonizing with my past, present, and future,
In ways I cannot begin to explain.

I had thought my life was destined
To be spent alone in the service of my God,
But the Principle Power that directs our lives
Had other plans, and brought us together
Forever in His presence, that we might bring
Praise and honor to His glorious name.

THE DAGGER'S EDGE

I implore of you, my jaded love,
That you salve the old wounds festering
From scorching words echoing in corridors;
Hot daggers piercing to the quick.

Bleeding casualties, and each alone
Suffering from harsh dark parting grief,
Crushed in pride; bereft of joyous bliss
Which one time seemed to us secure.

I implore of you, my jaded love,
That you savor the fond memories.
Budding love may still dispel the torment,
And dull the dagger's cutting edge.

LOVE REKINDLED

In this life
We do not always walk
In the joyous light of day.
Sometimes the night comes
When the moon is not visible
And the stars cannot be seen
Anywhere in the heavens.
We are left to grope
In darkness alone.

The night comes,
But there is always
The dawning of another day
And the restoration of
Joyous new light.
There follows the ecstasy
Of living and of being,
And the miracle
Of love rekindled.

MARRIAGE

What is there in life
That fills the human heart and soul
With greater joy than marriage?
What mortal promise, what pursuit,
What endeavor of men and women
Is so respectable, so praiseworthy,
So heavenly divine
As the institution of marriage?
What enterprise is so dear,
What success so pleasant,
What victory so sweet
As a long and happy marriage?
What else can lift the spirit so high,
Touch life so profoundly,
Nourish love so deeply?
What hope is so fond,
What faith so enduring,
What glory so great,
As the bond of matrimony
That fulfills all, delights all,
Endures all?

ON LIVING & ON DYING

RENDEZVOUS WITH LIFE

Though old and feeble with the years,
Though but a shadow of myself,
And though I would with few sad tears
Repose this book upon the shelf;

Where other volumes gather dust:
Where mold, decay, and mildew dwell
Among the pages dank and must,
Where pains subside, where sorrows quell;

To leave my friends behind, bereft;
To end this painful arduous strife --
But I still have a chapter left;
I have a rendezvous with life!

THE GLORY OF WAR

O person, O people, O nation of pride;
Your army, your navy, your force is your guide.
"The glory of war" your people have said,
But where is the glory for those who are dead?

Talk at the table, then talk once again;
Seek peaceful solutions, don't lose your good men.
Pursue every glimmer of hope for peace;
Stay cool and stay calm, let hostilities cease.

O people, O nation, O world of pride,
Your army, your navy, your force is your guide.
A harsh word spoken, an angry reply;
"The glory of war" is the hue and the cry.

A shot, then a skirmish; a wide open rift,
And retaliation is brutal and swift.
The cord is now broken, the horror begins:
Alas, it is war, and in war no one wins.

The death and destruction, the terror we loathe:
Soldiers, civilians, with casualties both.
Brutality reigns over reason once more;
Hideous and heinous, the glory of war.

Mindless the butchery and mindless the fear;
Mindless the hatred, the sword and the spear;
Senseless the cannon, the mortar and gun -
With no hope for justice found under the sun.

Pitted lands smoldering, scorched black and bare;
Desolate cities and towns everywhere.
A hellish pall hangs as a shroud from the sky,
The body count soars as they die, and they die.

O person, O people, O nation of pride,
Your army, your navy, your children have died.
"The glory of war" your people have said,
But where is the glory for those who are dead?

BENEATH THE SOD

Beneath the sod the bodies lie entombed
In caskets made of pine and ancient wood;
May they, at rest in peace, not be exhumed,
Though they would tell their stories if they could,
For buried with them is a mystery:
A life of int'rest, I am sure; untold -
A grand and noble part of history;
Of lives that shone to others as of gold
So polished and refined, that teardrops fell
As freely as the rain those dreary days
When these beloved souls came here to dwell,
Departing from this world's wicked ways:
Somehow I sense our lives were shaped by those
Who lie here quiet in these hallowed rows.

BENEATH NOVEMBER'S MOON

November winds exacerbate
October's dying breath,
With summer's life now ending
With such a chilling death.

But colors spilling from the trees,
From every shrub and bush;
Do pale the essence of July,
And flowers' vivid blush.

O, would that I could live my life
As April, May, and June,
And lay myself down quietly
Beneath November's moon.

ONLY COWARDS LEAP

I have stood on the mountain's steepest ledge,
Breathed the sweet air, sought respite;
Loveless, heart-broke, beckoned to the edge
Where oblivion welcomes darkest night
Without end; where all blessed mortals sleep.
A man like that carries a grudge,
But only cowards leap.

I have traveled along life's meager road,
Trod through the wastelands, pricked by thorn,
Thistles, briers, and bore the heavy load
To the point I wished I'd never been born:
Bleeding, bruised, and wounded deep.
A man like that will reap what's sowed,
But only cowards leap.

I have weathered storms on oceans wide,
Been cast about, and cast away;
Spurned, and turned all teary eyed
To look for just one friend that day,
Yet none would come to this black sheep.
A man like that will wish he'd died,
But only cowards leap.

I have wondered through both flood and drought:
Been washed quite clean, been covered black
With muck and grime, been filled with doubt,
Then took the road that brought me back
Where saints and sinners honor keep.
A man like that will cheer and shout,
But only cowards leap.

SHORTY

It's been near fifty years ago,
But I remember it like yesterday...
When a weak and spindly colt was born
In a wet and snowy spring;
Such gangly legs, and a small star
Plastered off-center on his too-big head,
"Not much good fer nuthin" Dad said.
Shorty proved us all wrong
With a heart the size of Gibralter
And a spirit of the restless west wind
Driving his legs and rippling shoulders;
Fully grown he would thunder
Across the pastures far ahead
Of the other "good" draft horses,
And hitched to the sod-plow
Shorty would pull twice his share,
And by nightfall when the
Other bigger ones were lagging
And their single-trees were sagging
He would pull the plow alone
And would have died rather than quit,
That's the kind of horse he was,
And in the early fall of sixty-three
He lit out of the barn in full stride
And ran into the end of a steel gate.
Li' Shorty came to a sudden end,
And I mourned for him as a man
Would mourn for his friend.

THE QUESTIONS I KEEP ASKING

Oh, the questions I keep asking are as subtle as the wind,
That keeps blowing o're the meadows off the Bay of Chesapeake;
Why do ordinary people keep a score of those who've sinned?
Why do men who ridicule never turn the other cheek?

Will the victims of tomorrow be the ones who've lost their fame?
Will the heroes of the city be the laughing stock of town?
Will the rising tide of envy frame the ones who've won the game?
Are the whispers I keep hearing merely words to put them down?

Oh, the questions I keep asking are as subtle as the pine
When the winter winds go whistling through the branches thick and thin;
Not a solitary moment when we do not hear the whine -
Hear the crying, hear the sighing, of what could and might have been.

Will the innocent mistake be turned to horror without scale?
Will the brother and the sister be beside themselves with shame?
Will the family be parted by those passing on the tale?
Will a little spark of fire now ignite a roaring flame?

Oh, the questions I keep asking are as subtle as the snakes,
That keep slithering and hissing through the grasses and the reeds;
Will the rumor mills keep grinding on about our worst mistakes?
Will the beauty of the flowers now be hidden by the weeds?

AS A LIGHTHOUSE STANDS

Stand, young man, as a lighthouse stands,
At the crest of a raging sea,
With a beacon light
On a moonless night
While the winds shriek mightily.

Moor yourself to a towering rock
Of truth and equity;
Be a reference guide
On the other side
Of the shoals of anarchy.

Hold your own when the going thing
On the tide of a mortal throng,
Is to play with shame
In a reckless game
Of ignoring right and wrong.

Stand young man, as a lighthouse stands
On the edge of a raging sea;
With your head held high,
With a fog horn cry
Leading on to victory.

OF WILLOW AND OF WREN

Had I the patience of the tree
Awaiting for the spring;
The busy-ness of honey bee
Who rests no weary wing.
Had I the humble gallantry
Of willow and of wren,
Without the pride and pageantry
The peacock shows the hen -
Then maybe I could live my life
Just one day at a time,
With worry and with jealous strife
Mere words within a rhyme.

SOCIAL ISSUES

BAD BILLY

Billy sits inside his house,
Afraid to talk, afraid to play,
Afraid of this and every day;
Afraid of what his dad might do
If he should dare to disobey.

Billy wishes he were good;
He tries to be, but he is bad.
He's always and forever bad.
Why else would he be so despised
And bruised and battered by his dad?

THE COOL DUDE

The Cool Dude wore a black beret;
Dark sun glasses on a cloudy day,
A leather jacket with a silver star,
Drove a '49 two-tone Pontiac car;
Had a red tattoo of a bleeding heart
In a green-black vase all broken apart,
And all the women from here to Howe
Would stop and look with a raised eye-brow
As the Cool Dude passed with his car top down,
And he whistled and waved from town to town,
And everyone knew when they saw young Jacques,
Here was a man made of steel and rock.

The Cool Dude played a saxophone,
He could make it wail in a soulful tone,
He could make it hum, he could make it sing,
Make it fly away: sail on a feathered wing,
And he wouldn't come back for a breath of air
Till the ladies gasped and the men did sware,
And everyone sighed when he finished the tune,
And he walked outside 'neath the autumn moon
With a kind of swagger and a kind of strut,
With a bouncing step and a bouncing butt,
And the women folk hung by his side in droves,
Like the mango trees in the Mexican groves.

Now the Cool Dude drank like a desert horse:
Two six-packs and Scotch, of course,
Washed down quick with a sour or two,
As he chewed on nuts and he nursed his brew,
But the way he drove his car that night
Wasn't too cool and wasn't too bright,
As he sped from town and around the curve,
And he lost his grip and he lost his nerve,
As he hit the brakes a little too late,
And he lost it all in a twist of fate,
As the Cool Dude died of a bleeding heart
With his green-black car all broken apart.

SONG OF THE LONELY HEART

The song within the lonely heart
Is sung in minor key
Discordant and slow,
As the pines in November sing
When the north winds blow,
And as the serf sings at low tide
In a morning sea.

The song within the lonely heart
Beneath the waning moon's
Remorseful rhythm:
As sung by sad coyotes
In search of anthem,
As sung by mateless whippoorwills,
Lone curlews, parting loons.

The song within the lonely heart
Accomp'nied by the harp,
Dulcimer and flute;
The piercing sounds of piccolo
And the pensive lute,
Sung as the cold iron bells toll
At noontime, flat and sharp.

The song within the lonely heart
Is sung invariably
In painful silence;
As clouds in drought accumulate
Without recompense
Save for a few late caterwauls
Of toneless revelry.

WHO WOULD GIVE DRUGS TO A CHILD?

There are smooth-talking shysters
And scandalous crooks,
Hucksters and cheaters
And dastardly shnooks,
All of them crime records
Filed a mile long;

But who would give drugs to a child?

There are wretched and miserable
Back-stabbing snitches,
Traitors and scoundrels
And infidel witches,
Quite reason enough to be
Riled the day long;

But who would give drugs to a child?

There are rude rabble-rousers
And ruffian types,
Snide and presumptuous
Persnickety-snipes;
No wonder they have not
Smiled for so long;

But who would give drugs to a child?

There are slanderous liars
And scalawag sorts,
Scum-bags and flea-bags
With all their cohorts,
No doubt they have been
Defiled all along;

But who would give drugs to a child?

THE MAN IN THE CARDBOARD BOX

There once lived a man in a cardboard box,
His ceiling and floors were made of rocks,
His bed was half a bale of hay,
Now that was all right, it was okay,
But he fumed and fussed, and swore, he did,
And behaved himself as a little kid,
'Cause the mice chewed holes in his cotton socks,
And his toes peeked out of his socks, they did.

He hung him some curtains of burlap bags,
And used for his carpets worn out rags,
And for his chair he used a crate;
"Now there" said he, "Now that's first rate!"
But he screamed and yelled, he stomped his feet,
And his faced turned red as a garden beet,
When a cat came by and she made her a nest
In his carpet rags by his first rate seat.

This man who once lived in a cardboard box
Soon built him a table of cinder blocks;
He made bouquets of dandelion,
And laughed out loud at things so fine;
But he shook his fist and whirled around,
And made an awful screeching sound
When a dog came by and he sniffed his box,
And he lifted his leg, and he wet the ground.

MONUMENT OF DEATH

A fragile and a delicate abode,
Where peasant and the noble born reside:
Where peacock shares the shade with horny toad,
Where scorpions and lions stalk beside
The flaming desert rose; where idle thorns
Indulge the carnal waters of the Nile,
Where sweet fruitful vines and grains adorn
The delta of the savage crocodile;
In such a place as this we live and weep,
For she forbears the brutish with the wise:
The lash of whips could never hurt as deep
As the ravaging by which she now dies -
And who among us shall be left to raise
A monument of death to profit's praise?

A PERSON IS A PERSON

Some have on a fancy suit, a fancy shirt and tie;
Some will smile and wave to you as you go walking by.
Some will hang their heads in shame, or give to you a frown;
Some will have a broken heart, or wear a tattered gown.

Some are cherished from the womb and dandled on the knee;
Some come from the best of homes where love is given free.
Some come from a broken home, some have no home at all;
Some have never known love, some face a prison wall.

Some will live a life of ease, of blissful peace and cheer;
Some have friends to help them out with not a thing to fear,
Some will be abused a bit and some will suffer pain;
Some live on the streets at night, and in the snow and rain.

So let's not hasten to condemn, or criticize, or hate;
For much of life, it seems depends, on fortune and on fate.
A person is a person, and not a beast or brute;
Judge a person by his heart and not his bitter root.

COMFORT AND CONDOLENCES

REST IN PEACE

At last, my friend, at last:
Thy raging sea no longer swells,
No anguish in thy bosom dwells,
No anxious thoughts or worried mind,
No bruised or bleeding wounds to bind,
No weariness from working late,
Nor loss of gain from twist of fate.
At last, my friend, at last;
You rest in peace at last.

Sleep well, my friend, sleep well:
Recline in deep and tranquil sleep,
No more thy tear-filled eyes shall weep,
No harmful vengeance on thee now,
No hindrance from a fevered brow,
No cold, no heat, can cause thee pain,
No drought can parch thy lips again.
Sleep well, my friend, sleep well;
In slumbering sleep well.

Be still, my friend, be still:
At peace depart as friend with friend,
No more travail with trouble send,
No stormy wind will take thy rest,
No sorrow pierce thy pulsing breast,
No angry words thy silence break,
No misery keep thee wide awake.
Be still, my friend, be still;
In restful sleep be still.

From warring factions find relief,
No turmoil hence to cause thee grief,
No strife for thee is now in store,
No more the unctuous threat of war,
No man, no beast, no thorny rose,
Nor noise can wake thy sure repose.
At ease, my friend, at ease;
In peaceful rest, at ease.

Farewell, my friend, farewell:
Farewell to thee as you depart,
No more thy vessel dashed apart,
No more thy hull awash on reefs,
No more thy shoals of life cause griefs,
No ill wind tear thy billowed sails,
No masts that snap before the gales.
Farewell, my friend, farewell;
Bon Voyage, farewell.

Revive, my friend, revive!
Awake and rise in cheerful song,
No grave can keep thy spirit long!
No chains that fetter thee can last,
No death can seize and hold thee fast!
For One there is who holds the key
That conquers death in victory!
Revive, my friend, revive;
Forever more, revive!

"DAD"

It was just a short while ago, Dad,
That we worked and we played by your side;
But the days, the months, the years sped by
As time can not be denied.
For the shadows of day would grow long, Dad,
And the sun would sink low in the west;
And the cold winter winds would blow, Dad,
And the birds take leave of their nest.

It's not just the hard work you did, Dad,
Through the heat of the day for us all,
And it's not just the things you gave us:
Winter, spring, summer, and fall.
It's the way you shared of your life, Dad,
With the loss of your sleep and your rest.
And it's the way you handled yourself, Dad,
When the rest of us weren't at our best.

It is not just the harvest of grain, Dad,
But the planting and care of the seed;
And it's not just the way you would scold us
Whenever we wouldn't heed -
It's the way that you felt of our pain, Dad;
From the harm in the things that we'd do.
It's the way you belonged to us, Dad,
It's the way we belonged to you.

All the times you suffered for us, Dad,
While you gave us the cheer of your song;
And now that you're no longer with us,
It seems that we often long
For the time we can see you again, Dad,
And to hear you laugh as we meet;
To talk of the times gone by, Dad,
As we sit at the table and eat.

MOTHER'S LOVE

No other memories endure the test of time
To fill with such abiding fondness still,
As the memories of Mother's love sublime;
May she rest in quiet peace upon the hill.

Until the sound of trumpets blasting rends the sky
And the Lord of hosts descends upon the earth,
To wipe away the tears of those who cry
And replace them with the tears of joy and mirth.

RESURRECTION

O Mortal shuck of lifeless grain
Laid to rest beneath the sod;
Betrothed to naught but dust and bane,
Moldering and fruitless pod.

O bright and shining Morning Star,
Living Spring of Deity;
Restore, refill this empty jar
With life for all eternity.

GIFTS TO BE TREASURED

She came as a gift to be treasured,
A trust to be guarded,
And a love to be cherished.
We heard her soft and gentle voice
In the evening of her life;
And we shared her laughter
At the dinner table,
But all too soon we saw
Her sun setting before our eyes.
We will take comfort
In knowing that she would
Not want us to mourn too long,
Nor grieve too deeply for her,
For she was a lover of good things,
And someone who looked
On the bright side of circumstances.
We will remember her
For the good things she brought us:
The kind words,
The loving moments,
The sweet memories -
Gifts to be treasured
Forever

MORNING BRINGS THE SUNSHINE

Lonely toll the bells of mourning
For the dear one gone before;
Lonely weary waves of sorrow
Sweep across the barren floor
Of the sad and unconsoled
Mate behind the loveless door;
Left to face the sad and dreary
Emptiness that's now in store.

Morning brings the lavish sunshine
Pouring through the window pane.
Songbirds fill the air with music;
Heavenly the sweet refrain.
God of mercy, God of pardon,
Fill this heart with Your delight;
Lift this continence with gladness
In the presence of your light.

MY BLOOD, MY BONES, MY BROTHER

Whose consolation can console,
Whose soul can sympathize;
Who can fill the gaping hole
When a dear brother dies?

When blood of blood, when bone of bones,
When flesh from whence it came;
Do rest beneath the stepping stones
Of life, and life the same.

For did not one with other share
The pattern on the loom;
The father and the mother's care,
The selfsame fertile womb?

MY SISTER, MY FRIEND

Sister - how I do miss you here!
How I miss of your pleasant cheer!
Your sharing and caring,
Your tender forbearing
That made you so loving and dear!

I shed of my tears and I cry,
And at night in my bed I sigh,
For the loss and the toll
On my heart and my soul,
Where lingering memories lie.

My sister, my dearest, my friend:
The pain of our parting will mend,
When we rise in the morn
Revived and reborn,
Where unspeakable joys never end!

THE SLEEPING SEED

For every flower, wilted, dying,
Many a seed there can be found:
Many a seed is left there lying
In the cold and listless ground.
From Each blossom that is leaving
Glorious blooms will reappear;
From each death that leaves us grieving
Comes the blossom full of cheer.

For the sun from heaven glowing
Beckons to the sleeping seed;
Calls the resting seed to growing
Glorious plant of rose or reed.
So the body we now bury
In this dark and dismal place,
Is a seed which shall here tarry
Still of life and still of grace.

Till the Son from heaven glowing
Sheds His light upon the earth,
And His awesome Spirit flowing
Shows this soul's inherent worth;
Thus the seed which rests here, dormant,
With no anguish, pain, or strife,
Will then spring forth free of torment
To eternal glorious life!

SERENITY

A COTTAGE SMALL

Would that I could find a place
Beside a trickling stream,
Where I could hear the waters sigh
And whisper while I dream.

Would that I could find a place
Within a sheltered glen,
Where birds could sing their lullabies
For weary older men.

Would that I could find a place
Beyond the city street,
Where wild flirtatious flowers scent
My Shangri-La retreat.

Would that I could find a place
To build a cottage small,
Where I could leave my cares behind,
And forget them, one and all.

SONNET OF PEACE

At even tide, when all is calm at last,
And I sit quiet 'neath the aspen shade,
With summer's sky in golden amber cast
Above my blissful verdant grassy glade:
Where wind-caressed red clover buds do spill
Their sweetly distilled perfume everywhere,
While cheerful leaves about me hum and trill,
And songs of birds festoon the magic air
With melodies so lovely heaven-sent
I seldom think a worried thought, or bring
To mind a dark and dreary sad moment,
And then it is my heart does gladly sing
And dance within my awed and humbled breast;
To contemplate of life so richly blest.

RURAL CHARM

Have you ever spent a summer;
Lazy summer on a farm?
With the cats and little kittens,
With the horses and their fittin's,
With the cattle and the calves
Out in the barn?

Have you heard the rooster crowing;
Loudly crowing come the dawn?
Have you seen the misty sunrise,
Pink and gold before your two eyes;
Shine in glory twixt the trees
Out in the lawn?

Have you ever trampled barefoot;
Reckless barefoot in the clay?
In the fresh-plowed dirt and diggin's;
On the clods, both small and big 'nes
Till they crumbled 'round your toes
So cool and gray?

Have you played upon a hay-mow;
Pungent hay-mow way up high?
Have you jumped and rolled and tumbled,
With your friends together jumbled
Till you laughed so hard you 'most
Commenced to cry?

Have you romped on country acres;
Country acres in the sun?
Have you waded knee-deep streams
Splashing cool as in your dreams,
Then went dipping with your clothes
Off just for fun?

Have you ever spent a summer;
Busy summer on a farm?
Chased a rat or chased a mouse;
Flushed a pheasant or a grouse,
And experienced rural living
With its charm?

THE VALLEY OF SAINT JOE

The Saint Joe River Valley
Is home sweet home to me.
My roots are there entangled
And there I long to be.

It's misty in the morning
When dew is on the ground;
The trees drip their honey wine
And sparkling gems abound.

The hazy morning sunshine
Soon filters through the pines;
Through cottonwoods, through maples,
And intertwining vines.

The breeze that's blowing softly
Whispering through the leaves,
So gently swoops and kisses
The grasses in the leas.

And soon the bees will gather
Their nectar to and fro,
Buzzing gaily everywhere
The flowers bloom and grow.

You can have your tinsel towns
And cities built for show;
I will build my cottage in
The Valley of Saint Joe.

O FOR A MOMENT

The lines of our lives are twisted and taut,
Our moorings un-tethered and tossed;
The stress and the strain of each day is bought
With a piece of tranquility lost.
O for a moment alone in the shade
Of an elegant oak, or a pine;
To rest on a log in a wooded glade
To untangle these heart-strings of mine.

The competitive edge in a business deal,
And a push to keep up with the Jones;
In a world gone mad with its misguided zeal
To consume my raw flesh with the bones.
O for a moment alone in the heights
With a blanket of stars overhead,
Raptured in awe at the symphonic lights
And the splendor of leaves for my bed.

The jangle of cars on the thoroughfare,
As I rush from hither to yon,
With the daily fetters of worry and care,
I could sing the encore of the swan.
O for a moment of quiet and peace
On the banks of a fresh water stream,
Far from the wake of the maddening pace
Where the quest runs away with the dream.

HOME IN KOSCIUSKO

In Kosciusko County
Stood a house of brick and wood,
There beside a well of water
Where there once a windmill stood;
Where the lilacs bloomed in springtime,
Where the crimson clover grew,
And the twining morning glories
Sparkled with the diamond dew.

There just off of road One Hundred,
South of Federal Highway Six,
On one hundred twenty acres,
With the horses, cows, and chicks;
There I grew from early childhood
To my later upper teens,
There I witnessed charm and beauty
In those glorious rural scenes.

There the gold finch and the robin
Made their home and kept their guard,
And the wren would build her nest
Out in the grape vines of our yard.
There the hawks would hunt for rodents,
And the martins soared the sky,
There the hoot owls kept their vigil
On their night posts from on high.

There I saw the U-creek meander
Through the early corn and wheat,
There I saw the maple growing,
Giving shade from summer heat;
There I saw the autumn colors,
The migration of the goose,
And I saw the winter snow
Clinging to the Norway spruce.

There my father and my mother
Raised all fourteen of their brood,
And it couldn't have been easy,
For it took a lot of food;
Back home in Kosciusko,
In that house of brick and wood -
In a home where both the parents
Did the best that parents could.

NATIVE AMERICA

AS A DREAM DIES

West to the land of the bleak reservation,
West to the land where the coyotes prowl;
West where the home river basin's a memory
That dies with the bison and lonely wolf's howl.

Cold is the wind from the lake Winnebago,
Cold is the ice and the snow on the dell;
Scant are the clothes of the women and children
Who trudge on the frozen lone highway to hell.

Death stalks the trail of the proud Indian nation,
The way to salvation still-frozen in red;
The Great Spirit turns His pale face in anguish
From corpse after corpse on a white feather-bed.

West to the land of the bleak reservation,
West to the land where the cockleburs grow;
West where the home river basin's a memory
That dies as a dream dies: as embers in snow.

AS THE RIVER FLOWS

As the river flows
with a mighty purpose
and cannot be stopped,
hindered, or held back,
so you, my child,
must live your life
with a mighty purpose,
with great resolve,
and with no regrets.

Let not the darkness
of the moonless night,
the cold winds of
the north lands,
nor the thunder clouds
of the far west,
keep you from achieving
your life's dreams.

As the river flows
swiftly over the cleft rock,
and rushes past the
steep hills of the forest;
and beneath the cold
ice of the winter;
never looking back
with regret at what
is left behind,
so let your eyes

always look forward
to tomorrow; and not
back to yesterday's
barriers, setbacks,
sorrows, and detours.

Let the full moon
and the stars of heaven
ever be your guide,
let the sun shine
warm upon your face,
let the rain quench
your burning thirst,
and eat only what
the good earth gives you
for the day, nothing more.

Always be a friend to
the wolf and the bear,
learn the wisdom of
the crow and the hawk,
and let your life
flow like the river
flows to the great sea;
and you, my child,
will always be at
home where ever
you make your bed.

HOWL OF THE SHE-WOLF

(Semi-Sestina)

The darkness flees when eastern skies
Send forth the gleam of amber gold.
The earth turns white when northern winds
With anguishing and mournful howls
Blow clouds of snow that drift away
Across the meadows pillow soft.

Beyond the hills the she-wolf howls,
Her pups alone, her pack away.
Her echoes reach across the soft
And snowy vales beneath the skies
Of pink and amber, blue and gold;
Her tracks dispersed by gusty winds.

Across the river far away
The wolf pups cry, and sniff the winds
Beneath the rising sun of gold
For scent of milk. In search of soft
Protective coat; alert for howls
The she-wolf casts into the skies.

The morning sun bursts forth in gold
To spread her amber glowing soft
Beneath the vast horizon skies
Upon the dell: To chase away
The chill of night, and warm the winds
That carry forth the plaintive howls

Upon the snowy wings of winds,
Upon the devil bird in skies
That shriek and wail - to follow howls
In search of game and coins of gold,
In search of trophy wolf skins soft...
The hunters come from far away.

Alone and lost, and whimp'ring soft,
The hungry pups can hear no howls;
Not near to them, not far away;
No mother's scent upon the winds...
The stillness steals across the skies
But coldly clink the coins of gold.

The morning skies have lost their gold,
The evening winds moan low and soft,
And far away, no she-wolf howls.

COME TO US

Ode to Native America

Come to us,
O wind of the north,
Blowing from the hills and vales,
Touch us with your breath of yesterday
When the skies were young and
The tall virgin prairie grasses
Fed the never-ending herds
Of bison: life to a people
At one with this land -
Come to us.

Come to us,
O rain of the east,
Flowing from the highlands;
Wash us with your cleansing laughter
To lift our spirits to our fathers
And mothers before us,
Who gave us our lives,
And taught us to
Love all of life -
Come to us.

Come to us,
O sun of the south,
Shining as a fire in the skies,
Warm us with your kiss of regeneration
To propagate the trees, plants,
Beasts, and beings of earth.
Fill us with your brightness
So we may find our way
In this dark world -
Come to us.

Come to us,
O land of the west,
Stretching to the heights
As a free land to a brave people,
Rolling out before us as a great
Habitation of hopefulness,
A home for the wounded
Pride of the old nations
Pushed to the brink -
Come to us.

HOME OF THE NATIVE

Our home is where the prairie meets the sky:
Where bison roam, and wolves give birth to pups,
Where eagles soar, where hawks and night owls fly,
Where pristine flowing rivers fill our cups,
Where winds can sweep the dust to distant lands
And bring the rain clouds rolling overhead;
Where brothers dance within their Native bands
And moon beams light the eyes of newlywed.
All land is free for creatures small and great,
And reaches where horizon never ends:
For deer, the bear, the brave, and to his mate -
The eagle and the crow are viewed as friends.
Our home is where the prairie meets the sky;
May I be free to live there till I die.

THE TIPPECANOE

Weaving through the countryside
In a thread of green and blue,
Is a wonderful part of the Hoosier land;
The beautiful Tippecanoe.

Serenading through the mist
To the song of the water-flow;
The mystical song that the river sang
To the Indians long ago.

Shimmering art reflected here
In a frame of crystal dew,
Is naught but the art of the Master's hand
On the beautiful Tippecanoe.

HOW TO RATE AND JUDGE POETRY

HTR&JP system by M. L. Hochstetler

This system of judging and rating poetry can be helpful to all who wish to judge poetry on the merits. These judging guidelines are written to help determine which poems should be highly esteemed, and selected as the top choices in poetry contests. It is based on a 100 point system, with the highest possible score being 100 points. Ten areas are listed which can be rated from 1 to 10 points. Each category is listed and explained below.

(1). BEAUTY, POWER, EDUCATION, or ENTERTAINMENT

At the very least all poems need one of the following four values (highest possible total - 10) and if it has more than one of these, so much the better:

BEAUTY - either in the combinations of descriptive and colorful language, beautiful word pictures, the beauty in the thoughts that are evoked; such as serenity, idealism, inspiration, or perhaps even beauty in general appearance, as it looks on paper: not disjointed, disconnected, or disorganized in appearance. Some poems are made to appear on paper as the subject that is being described: for instance - a lamp, an hour glass, a tree, a sail, a loaf of bread, etc. (see Royal Debonair – page 4 of this book for an example). This, in itself, if the writer has done a good job, should be worth extra points.

POWER - a powerful poem is one that stirs you, hits you square between the eyes, lifts you up emotionally, makes feel good inside, or takes you, the reader, into the depths of sorrow and pathos, flaming anger, or bitter disappointment, along with the author. It may lift you up mentally and take you to exotic or far off places, or takes you back in time and place you squarely in the middle of some cataclysmic or earth-shaking event (such as Lord Byron's "Charge of the Light Brigade" for instance. One way to gage the power of a poem is to gage the emotional impact it has on you: does it move you to tears? Does it make you angry? Or perhaps you feel awestruck, overjoyed, or sorrowful. Do you long to be at the place the poem describes? EDUCATION - does the poem have educational value? The "Charge of the Light Brigade" is really a very beautiful poem, written in powerful language, and has educational value all at the same time. It is based on a true historical event. So you can see where these three factors should cause us to rate this poem highly, using these three criteria. However, we shouldn't necessarily assume a poem has no educational value just because it is not based on true events. The events may be plausible, hypothetical, give us a valuable lesson, or moral, and have great educational value even if it is fictional. Also, keep in mind, just because a poem has good educational value does not give it license to reject beauty. Beauty and power should be of paramount importance, along with education or entertainment, depending on the purpose of the poem.

ENTERTAINMENT - does the poem have entertainment value? If it is not in some way beautiful, powerful, or educational, then it must, at the very least, serve to entertain us in some way. This could include such things as humor, irony, rhyming riddles, mystery, drama, horror, science fiction, and satire.

Using the criteria listed above, I would have to give *"Charge of the Light Brigade"* a perfect 10, because in reality, Lord Byron's poem uses all four of these masterfully in his classic poem. Beauty, power, and education are given to us in a delightfully entertaining manner. However, a poem doesn't necessarily have to have all four to rate a perfect 10 in this category.

(2) FUNCTIONALITY & INTEREST:

The functionality and interest level of a poem are related to how well it achieves its intended purpose while maintaining the interest level in the poem. Ask yourself: Is the message clear? Does the poem serve a good purpose, or is it of little value to anyone? Is the message profound, or is it trite? A poem that deals with trivial matters or concerns should not rate as highly in this category, unless it is of keen interest to the majority of people in society. "Love" is not a trivial matter, whereas your own personal love life may be a trivial matter to others. On the other hand, it may be of great interest to others, depending on how it is written. Ask yourself: "Does the poem work, or is there something not quite right? Maybe the words sound "forced" in a rhyming poem, or trite and predictable in a free-verse poem. In his poem "Little Orphant Annie" James Whitcomb Riley grabs your interest from the start, and carries it on through the entirety of the poem.

You must rate the poem fairly, even if the topic or subject of the poem is not something of particular interest to you. Let's say you hate the game of golf, and you were asked to judge the merits of a humorous poem on golf. You would have to ask yourself, "would somebody who likes the game find this poem of great interest?" and rate the poem accordingly. If you cannot see where the poet gets his message across in an interesting, clear, and a unique way, is of little importance to anyone, or the interest level would be low to you and most others, then you would have to give the poem a low score in this area. Poems with profound concepts, unforgettable "punch lines" or conclusions, should be given extra credit. Give an honest evaluation, and score between 1 and 10.

(3) EXPERTISE & TECHNICAL CORRECTNESS

Is the poem riddled with grammatical errors, misspelled words, double negatives, or wrong punctuations? Is the poem crafted to form the desired poetic style, such as a Sonnet, a Ballad, a lyric, a free verse, a Haiku, a Tonka, or a limerick? Does it substitute "your" for "you're," "there" for "they're" or "alter" for "altar"? If so, it needs to be graded accordingly. These types of mistakes also take away from the beauty of the poem, so you would need to dock points from the first category as well. However, keep in mind that technical expertise is more than using the proper form, grammar, and spelling. It also includes the way the poem is organized and how the thoughts are presented. Is it titled appropriately? Should the lines be shortened? Is there a proper "economy" of thoughts and words? Should the overall poem have been shortened and streamlined? Does it reveal too much and leave nothing to the imagination, or does it not reveal enough? Perhaps there should be another "fill in" verse, or perhaps there is no proper concluding verse. Does it look polished and professional? Sometimes giving a poem extra time will reveal to us what it needs or what it lacks. I have written poems in the past which I thought were excellent at the time I wrote them, but the same poems have since been either totally rewritten, or relegated to the trash pile. If a poem is technically correct and appears well polished, give it the full 10 points.

(4). RHYME and/or METER

Poems don't have to rhyme to rate highly in this category, but if the poem is written as rhyming verse, then it should be rated according to how well the rhymes fit, not only with each other, but with the flow and the intended meaning of the verse. Read and study the rhymes in Henry Wadsworth Longfellow's Poem "The Builders" as an excellent example of good rhyming verses, with beautiful cadence. A poem must have some sort of acceptable meter (rhythm or cadence). Meters/rhythms can alternate from verse to verse and from line to line, but they should form a pattern to create a pleasing effect. Even in free verse, the words must create their own pleasant rhythm, and not clash with each other, cause clumsy pauses, twist the tongue, or put the emphasis in the wrong places.

An excellent example of good rhyme and meter, with an emotional ending, is found in Edna St. Vincent Millay's poem "The Ballad of the Harp-Weaver." Notice how the words are phonetically pleasing, the rhymes are excellent, and the syllables in the words create a natural and pleasant rhythm, even though the rhyme itself is sad. This creates a most satisfying emotional experience for the reader, and is more pleasing than just a collection of sad thoughts on a page.

(5) ASSONANCE

Assonance has to do with the pleasing and proper sound of the words, and word-sounds that interact with other words and fit the poem's mood. A good example of pleasing assonance is found in Edgar Allan Poe's "The Bells" in which you can almost hear the various bells sounding throughout the poem. Another good example of using vowels and consonants to good advantage is found in the poem "Lincoln, Man of the People" by Edwin Markham, where the author uses powerful words to express powerful thoughts. In tranquil, or pastoral type poems, you would want to use totally different sounds, using such words as: softly, peacefully, quietly, hushed, etc. Ask yourself, does the poem use the proper sounds for the subject matter? In describing a peaceful setting you would not want to hear a lot of "snap, crackle, and pop" sounds. In describing a battle, one wouldn't think of using a lot of soft and placid sounds. For excellent sound quality (assonance) give the poem up to ten additional points.

(6) FORM & FLOW

The "form" of the poem simply is the shape the poem takes on paper: short lines or long lines, broken into verses, or left as an unbroken chain. Normally, a poet would strive to keep some kind of pleasant symmetry and balance in his verses; keeping corresponding lines close to the same length, so that each verse appears similar in size and shape to the rest. Also, it is not good to have a "bristled" appearance to your poem, where some lines stick out like misplaced bristles, giving it an unpolished and "skewered" or "lopsided" appearance. On the other hand, if the poem is about porcupines, or disheveled hair, a "bristled" or "hairy" appearance may be quite appropriate.

I recommend looking at Walt Whitman's poem "O Captain! My Captain" as an example of beautiful form in poetry. Also study the balance in the verses of Henry Wadsworth Longfellow's poem "The Builders." These are just two examples, among many of the Classics, which we can learn from. However, do not penalize a writer for creating unique and original form and shape in poetry, if there is a redeeming quality about it.

Flow has to do with the natural progression of the poem, both in thought and in speed, through natural pauses, or the lack of pauses. A serene setting should flow slower than a poem such as "Charge of the Light Brigade." Certain emotions should cause the poem to move faster: anger, hatred, fear in the heat of battle, a desperate fight for survival, etc. On the other hand, tranquility, satisfaction, benevolence, condolences, and love (unless it is an exciting experience) lend themselves to a slower "flow" of thoughts and events. A proper and professional balance in the above (No. 6) attributes should give a poem up to 10 points in any evaluation.

(7) OVERALL IMPACT

Overall impact is the ability of the poem to etch itself into your memory and your psyche. A poem may be beautifully written, be technically correct in every way, and have good rhyme, meter, flow, and form, and still not be a great poem. What makes a poem truly great is its ability to get under your skin, or to be so delightful as to be virtually unforgettable.

The difference, then, between a "good" poem and a truly exceptional, or "great" poem, is how deeply it affects you, and how long it holds you in its clutches after you are done reading it; not necessarily during the time you are reading it! If you can read the poem, and forget about it, then the poem did not have a great overall impact on you, and probably won't on others either. I would give very few poems 10 points in this category, even among the "classics" in literature. This is one area where you can, and should, be brutal in your evaluation. One other consideration is the age of the author. If a young child writes an exceptional poem, we may want to allow the age itself to "impact" us.

(8) CHOICE OF WORDS & READABILITY

As a judge, ask yourself whether the poem uses the best choice of words in the poem. Assonance has to do with using the best sounding words, but here we are talking of using the words with the best nuance of meaning. Here is where a rhyming poem could be severely penalized. The words used to make the best rhyme may not necessarily be the best choice of words to convey the idea, or the emotion you are trying to get across. A car can be going "fast," it can "speed" past you, "zip" or "zoom" by, or seem to "fly" past you at break-neck speed. Maybe it should "roar" past, which not only insinuates speed, but indicates a loud noise. As a judge of the poem, you need to decide if the author has used the best possible word or phrase to get the idea across.

The choice of words a poet uses should be geared toward the audience the poem is intended to reach. A poem for a young child would certainly not include a lot of college level language, nor should it have profanity, or vulgarity. A religious poem, intended for religious audiences, should not be crass and vulgar, or use anti-God slogans. Bigotry and racial slurs should be left out of all poems. A poem written for senior citizens should not denigrate old age. In general, all poems written for the public should show proper respect and honor to the races, ages, ethnic back grounds, sexes, and religions of all people.

I feel that too much criticism has been dished out on the poor old over-used and hack-kneed "cliché`. If the cliché` fits, and makes your poem work, then use it. After all, every word we use in day-to-day communication is a "cliché`" of sorts. Many phrases are repeated time and time again, does that mean we should never use them? A few examples are "green grass," "South wind," "morning sun," "cloudy sky," "garden fence," "winding road," "waves of the sea," "flower garden," and we could list hundreds more. A cliché is just a familiar and descriptive saying or phrase which is commonly used in society. We don't reject familiar and commonly used words in poetry, and neither should we reject phrases just because they are in common use. At times I have been criticized for using the cliché "happy as a lark" in my poem "A Fruitful Yield". I used it because it makes the poem work.

If I would have written "happy as a wren," happy as a monkey" or "happy as a chipmunk" it would not have had the same impact, and would have degraded the poem. Sometimes old familiar phrases work much better than original ones. However, one should always take care to use these phrases sparingly, and if an original word or phrase works well, then it should be used.

After you have checked the author's choice of words and phrases, read a few verses out loud. Does it read easily, with the periods, commas, accents and syllables flowing naturally, creating the proper tempo for the subject matter? Are there areas within the poem which seem to "trip" your tongue? Is it "readable" out loud for the average person? An excellent choice of words by the author, along with good readability, should add up to ten points in evaluating the poem as a whole.

(9) ORIGINALITY

Are the thoughts and phrases of the poem the author's, or are they borrowed from someone else's writings? I'm not referring to outright plagiarism, but the author may not be creating any new or unusual phrases of his own. Are the rhymes original, perhaps even unusual? Extra points should also be given to a poet who creates his own style in the rhythm and rhyming patterns of a poem. Rhymes don't always have to be at the end of each line, nor do thoughts and sentences have to end at the end of a line, or even a verse. Sentences and commas can be used effectively within lines to create unique and unusual pause patterns. Study some of Emily Dickinson's poems to see how expertly she carried thoughts and sentences from one verse to the next. She was also very gifted at coining original phrases in comparing one thing with something else. A poet needs to be given extra points for originality in subject matter, phraseology, rhyme, rhythm, and style. For an unusual poem, with extraordinary expressions, grant as many as 10 points.

(10) REASON

You have heard the expression "without rhyme or reason." Many modern poets, publishers, and judges, take great delight in praising extreme deviations from the more traditional and classical styles of poetry; so far extreme, in fact, that the common person cannot get any enjoyment from their supposed "masterpieces." It reminds a person of some of our modern art, which is mere design and color on paper. The modern trend in poetry has been moving toward poetry written without any "rhyme or reason." Some write mere word patterns and word resonances on paper, perhaps with meter patterns, and perhaps without, but poems devoid of any real reason or purpose, other than to create word patterns, has very little to offer anyone.

While there are good poems full of dark and mysterious phrases, and some are written as riddles or metaphors, poems should not leave a person feeling empty and totally perplexed as to the purpose and intent of the author. The "reason" or "reasoning" within the poem should be such that the reader can gain adequate knowledge of the message being relayed, or the purpose of the poem, even if it is for entertainment only. Is the poem too "economic" in portraying its intended message? Perhaps the poem is written as a metaphor, or its purpose is to keep the writer in suspense, but it should be concluded in a way that the reader understands that the poet is writing for mere entertainment, or in riddles, parables, and metaphors,

The purpose of the poem may to inspire, to lift up emotionally, to paint a word picture of a beautiful area, to give you something to look forward to, or to entertain, Many poems draw attention to serious social issues and problems. Poems can lambaste a great injustice, bludgeon it to death head on, or write about the problem from a much more subtle approach, which might be considered a more "reasonable" approach, and merit extra points. The purpose of an author may be to get a moral across, to eulogize a loved one, or remind you of how things were when he or she was a young child. Reason has to do with the "common sense" or the "clarity" by which the poet makes his points, and with how effectively the message gets across. Does the author merely "reason" off the top of his/her head, without giving you proof? If the poem is based on the personal experience of the author, this may be enough, where it might be totally inadequate when dealing with sensitive social issues. Does the author employ shallow reasoning? Does the author express feelings of anger and frustration, but leave you wondering why? Take all this into consideration before scoring up to ten points in this category.

Each of the above ten areas are critical in the creation of a quality poem. Once you have rated a poem in the ten categories listed, add the scores of each category to get an overall rating of the poem. Hopefully, this rating system will help you in judging, and in deciding which poets and which poems should be given a chance to win a contest.

Category	points
(1) BEAUTY, POWER, EDUCATION, or ENTERTAINMENT	10
(2) MESSAGE & INTEREST	10
(3) EXPERTISE & TECHNICAL CORRECTNESS	10
(4) RHYME and/or METER	10
(5) ASSONANCE	10
(6) FORM & FLOW	10
(7) OVERALL IMPACT	10
(8) CHOICE OF WORDS & READABILITY	10
(9) ORIGINALITY	10
(10) REASON	10
Total possible points	100

CPSIA information can be obtained
at www.ICGtesting.com
Printed in the USA
BVHW030719060422
633481BV00008B/13/J